BFS7/F7

1·1/0

Repentance and Revolt:
A Psychological Approach to History

Repentance and Revolt
A Psychological Approach to History

Richard Freeman

Rutherford • Madison • Teaneck
Fairleigh Dickinson University Press

Associated University Presses, Inc.
Cranbury, New Jersey 08512

SBN: 8386 7471 2
Printed in the United States of America

Contents

Preface

No doubt, many of us who study history share a deep curiosity as to why societies have differed, at times, considerably, from each other. They have contrasted not only with respect to their religion and culture, but also with regard to their political institutions, social structures, and foreign and imperialistic policies. Because of our curiosity, we are induced to ask certain pertinent questions. For example, why, until recently, were some advanced societies ruled by monarchs or military aristocracies, whereas others, even from earlier times, have been guided by commercial and industrial groups acting through parliaments? Why, in the present century, did some societies become communistic, some fascistic, and others avoid establishing rigidly centralized regimes? Why, throughout the ages, have certain societies surpassed others in their inclination to wage war and in the extent of their cruelty to subject peoples?

Admittedly, a number of historians have tried to account for these differences. Those belonging to the romantic school have attributed them to "leadership" or to "national character"; those adhering to the Marxian school have claimed that stages in economic development and in the dialectic are the causes. But these interpretations do not seem adequately to have explained the contrasts.

This book is an attempt to account for them. While taking into consideration the geographic and economic circumstances of the societies concerned, I stress the psy-

7

chological background. In this work, I try to show how
the psychological factors of fear, apprehension, obsession
with status, aggression, guilt feelings, and the need for a
sense of belonging—have all entered into the great drama
of history and created its many exciting but frequently
tragic episodes.

Quite possibly, an understanding of these psychological
factors can enable man to learn from the mistakes of his
past and be assured of a brighter future.

Acknowledgments

The author would like to thank the following publishers:

George Allen & Unwin, Ltd., for permission to quote from *The Trojan Women of Euripides,* translated by Gilbert Murray, 1919. *Nihongi,* translated by W. G. Aston, 1956. Friedrich Nietzsche, "The Will to Power," translated by A. M. Ludovici, from *The Complete Works,* edited by Oscar Levi, 1919.

The Barrie Group of Publishers, (Barrie Books Ltd.) for permission to quote from George Sansome, *A History of Japan to 1334,* 1958.

George Bell & Sons, Ltd., for permission to quote from Michel de Montaigne, "Of Repentance," from *The Essays,* Charles Cotton's translation edited by C. Carew Haslitt in Bohn's Library, in *Great Books of the World,* 1952.

Cambridge University Press, for permission to quote from G. C. Coulton, *Life in the Middle Ages,* in four volumes, 1930. (No. 5 published in paperback, in two volumes.)

Chatto & Windus, Ltd., for permission to quote from *Petrarch's Secret,* translated by W. H. Draper, 1911.

The Clarendon Press, Oxford, for permission to quote from "Politics," translated by Benjamin Jowett, from *The Oxford Translation of Aristotle,* edited by W. D. Ross, 1921, and from Benedetto Croce, *A History of Italy 1871–1915,* translated by Cecilia M. Ady, 1929.

Columbia University Press, for permission to quote from

9

Sources of the Japanese Tradition; Sources of the Chinese Tradition; and *Sources of the Indian Tradition,* from *Introduction to Oriental Civilization,* in *Records of Civilization: Sources and Studies,* edited by W. T. de Bary, 1958.

Constable & Company Limited, for permission to quote from Heinrich von Treitschke, *Politics,* in two volumes, translated by Blanche Dugdale and Torben de Bille, 1916.

J. M. Dent & Sons Ltd and E. P. Dutton & Co., Inc. for permission to quote from, in the Everyman's Library Series, "The Venerable" Bede, *The Ecclesiastical History of the English Nation,* translated by Stevens, revised by J. A. Giles, 1958. Samuel Johnson, *The Rambler,* 1953. J. J. Rousseau, *The Social Contract and Discourses,* translated by W. F. Trotter, 1946. John Stuart Mill, *Utilitarianism, Liberty and Representative Government,* 1944. Thomas B. Macaulay, *Speeches on Politics and Literature,* 1917.

E. P. Dutton & Co., Inc., for permission to quote, in the United States, from Feodor Dostoevsky, *The Possessed,* in two volumes, in the Everyman's Library Series, translated by Constance Garnett, 1960.

Fortress Press, for permission to quote from *The Works of Martin Luther,* translated by C. M. Jacobs, J. J. Schindel, A. T. W. Steinhaeser and W. A. Lambert, 1916.

Government of India, Publications Division, Ministry of Information & Broadcasting, for permission to quote from D. C. Sircar, *Inscriptions of Ashoka,* 1957.

Harvard University Press, for permission to quote from *Continuity and Change in Russian and Soviet Thought,* edited by Ernest J. Simmons, 1953.

William Heinemann, Ltd, for permission to quote from Leo Tolstoi, *The End of the Age,* translated by V.

Tchertkoff and I. F. Mayo, 1906. And, in the British Commonwealth and Empire, from Feodor Dostoevsky, *The Possessed,* translated by Constance Garnett, 1914.

Kenkyusha Limited, for permission to quote from Inazo Nitobe, *Lectures on Japan,* 1936.

Little, Brown and Company, for permission to quote from George Bancroft, *History of the United States of America,* in six volumes, 1876.

The Loeb Classical Library, for permission to quote from Virgil, *Works,* in two volumes, translated by H. Rushton Fairclough, 1956. Epictetus, *The Discourses as Reported by Arrian, the Manual and Fragments,* in two volumes, translated by W. A. Oldfather, 1946. Prudentius, *Works,* in two volumes, translated by H. J. Thomson, 1949.

The Macmillan Company, for permission to quote from K. S. Latourette, *The Chinese: Their History and Culture,* 1947. Edwin A. Robinson, *Collected Poems,* 1954.

Macmillan & Co. Ltd., for permission to quote from Henry Osborn Taylor, *The Medieval Mind,* in two volumes, 1914.

John Murray, for permission to quote from Richard Tawney, *Religion and the Rise of Capitalism,* 1927.

The Nonesuch Press, for permission to quote from Walt Whitman, *Complete Poetry, Selected Prose and Letters,* edited by Emory Holloway, 1938.

W. W. Norton & Company, Inc., for permission to quote from James Westfall Thompson and Edgar Nathaniel Johnson, *An Introduction to Medieval Europe, 300–1500.* Copyright, 1937, by W. W. Norton & Company, Inc.

The Pareto Fund, San Francisco, California, for permission to quote from Vilfriedo Pareto, *The Mind and Society,* in four volumes, translated by Andrew Bongiorno and Arthur Livingston, 1935.

Princeton University Press, for permission to quote from Desiderius Erasmus, *The Praise of Folly,* translated by H. H. Hudson, 1941.

SCM Press Ltd, for permission to quote, in the British Commonwealth and Empire, from Martin Luther, *Letters of Spiritual Counsel,* in *Library of Christian Classics,* published in the U.S.A., by The Westminster Press, 1957.

Charles Scribner's Sons, for permission to quote from James H. Breasted, *The Dawn of Conscience,* 1934.

The Westminster Press, for permission to quote, in the United States, from Martin Luther, *Letters of Spiritual Counsel,* in *Library of Christian Classics.* Published in the U.S.A. by The Westminster Press.

Yale University Press, for permission to quote from John Milton, "A Second Defense of the English People," translated by Helen North, from *Complete Prose Works,* in four volumes, 1966; Vol. IV, 1650–1655, Part I, edited by Don M. Wolfe.

The author also wishes to express his appreciation to Dr. Lin Yutang for permission to quote from his book *My Country and My People,* 1935.

Repentance and Revolt:
A Psychological Approach to History

1

The Origin of Fear,
Anxiety, and Taboo

A. The Emotion of Fear as Basic in All Animals, Including Man

All living things, from the lower to the higher orders, react to their surroundings, and their reactions are either toward or away from the particular habitat. This tendency to respond in the one way or the other is especially noticeable in the animal kingdom. All animals move toward or away from a situation, depending upon whether it is favorable or unfavorable. All of them seek places where they can satisfy their basic needs and avoid or escape from those that might be sources of danger.

By behaving in this way animals approach that which is friendly and familiar and avoid that which is unfamiliar. Why? Because life is a slow and continuous process of adapting to and becoming familiar with the surroundings. Adaptation leads to familiarity, and familiarity, to ever greater adaptation. That is, provided the environment itself remains comfortable and familiar. But should the surroundings suddenly change, what would happen? The animals experiencing this change would receive a shock. Immediately, they would be aware of something unfamiliar and posing as a threat to their security.

What circumstances could create such a shock? One would be a sudden lightening or darkening of the atmosphere; another, a rapid change of temperature; still another, an instant loud noise or feeling that the earth is moving from beneath. Any one of these conditions could startle an animal and cause fear.

Is man, the most highly developed animal, also startled by such circumstances? Definitely. We know only too well how a flash of lightning or a clap of thunder can create fear among children and even among adults, and how an explosion or earthquake can cause a panic in large crowds. These adverse circumstances, sudden and frightening, pose as threats to the persons experiencing them, and society recognizes them as potential dangers.

B. Anxiety and Taboo as Prevalent in Man

However, there is one frightening circumstance that everyone has experienced, but which society recognizes as being necessary for the survival of the human race. This is the act of being born, which, as the Austrian psychoanalysist Otto Rank was first to maintain, is a shocking experience for the individual undergoing it.[1] For birth entails the sudden lightening of the atmosphere and an instant loud noise, as well as the first attempt at breathing. Birth means a sudden thrust into unfamiliar surroundings. It thus creates fear.

All living things which are nervous and sensitive, in effect, the higher animals, experience fear at birth. Furthermore, those whose mental faculties are most highly developed subconsciously remember this frightening episode. Rank contended that this episode becomes traumatic, and that thereafter every strange situation causes fear. Gradually anxiety develops within the individual higher animal.

This is certainly the case with the human species. Man,

1. Otto Rank, *The Trauma of Birth,* London, 1929.

beset by anxiety, looks upon all unfamiliar circumstances as potential sources of danger. In fact, any event which he does not fully understand he regards with awe. It is here that we have the origin of taboo, so prevalent among primitive and, to a less extent, advanced peoples. By placing a taboo between himself and the mystery confronting him, man is freed from anxiety concerning it. That is why taboo is so widespread.

2

Taboos Among Primitive Peoples: The Basis of Future Asceticism

A. Taboos Relating to Sex and the Life Cycle

As we have noted, man has a deeply rooted anxiety about the unknown. Such anxiety is felt even more by primitive man than by his civilized contemporaries, because he knows less about the world, and every strange happening creates within him much greater alarm. Primitive man, burdened with anxiety, adheres to countless taboos, and the more anxious he feels about a particular circumstance, the greater his number of taboos concerning it.

Causing special anxiety among primitive peoples are happenings which are both mysterious and supposedly unclean. Such would be those relating to sex and the life cycle: puberty, menstruation, sexual intercourse, childbirth, and death. Therefore, it is in connection with these phenomenal occurrences that they have established peculiar prohibitions.

It is well known that primitive folk regard the facts of puberty and menstruation with great apprehension. Hence, they isolate adolescents going through this phase, fearing that they would harm themselves or others in the tribe.

Among the Winnebago Indians, women who are menstruating have to retire to a special lodge, where they remain in a sitting position. They are forbidden to look at any member of the tribe or even outdoors. Should they happen to, the person seen by them would supposedly experience a misfortune, or else the weather would become stormy. They have to abstain from food and water and cannot even touch their own bodies.[1]

The Nandi of Kenya consider all women who reach the age of puberty to be unclean. Thus, they shave the heads of pubescent girls and cover them with masks, while throwing long garments over their bodies. The purification ceremony is over only after the girls have walked four times under the surface of a pool, stream, or river.[2]

Needless to say, since puberty and menstruation are occasions for anxiety, so likewise is the sexual act itself. Hence, there are numerous restrictions and prohibitions associated with sexual intercourse.

The Zuñi Indians prohibit all sexual activity during and for several days following religious ceremonies. In fact, during these rituals members of the opposite sex are forbidden even to see each other.[3] The Nootka of Vancouver Island believe that all men engaged in whale fishing should not undertake such a venture unless they have abstained from intercourse with their wives for several months.[4] Among the Kiwai Papuans men about to go to war remain secluded from women, fearing that if they are intimate with them they, the men, will be killed.[5] The Bagatla of Bechuanaland think that persons who are sexually active have "hot blood"; in such a condition they should not have intercourse with ordinary people, whose health they might seriously impair.[6] The Thonga of South Africa forbid married couples to have contact with

1. Hutton Webster, *Taboo*, Stanford University, 1942, p. 91.
2. A. C. Hollis, *The Nandi*, Oxford, 1909, pp. 90–92.
3. Webster, *Taboo*, p. 138.
4. G. M. Sproat, *Scenes and Studies of Savage Life*, London, 1868, p. 227.
5. G. Landtman, *The Kiwai Papuans of British New Guinea*, London, 1927, p. 224.
6. Webster, *Taboo*, pp. 130–31.

those who are either ill or suffering from an injury; the mere presence of these matrimonial partners could cause death.[7]

From apprehension over sexual intercourse it is but one step to having similar anxiety about childbirth; on this occasion, too, primitive societies have established taboos.

Some tribes impose restrictions particularly on the male parent. The Bechuana of South Africa forbid a father from going hunting or even entering his own house two months after the birth of his child.[8] The Carib Indians of Guiana require that the father be a near slave to an older man during the months preceding his wife's delivery.[9] Other societies, however, regard the prospective mother as being more dangerous. The Kurovar of Malabar seclude a woman for twenty-eight days after her "first pains." During that time no one gives her any assistance; medicine is thrown to her, since all persons avoid direct contact. Following delivery both she and her husband must be purified by "holy water."[10] The Ba-ila of Rhodesia believe that if a pregnant woman approaches a tree it will lose its fruit; if she enters a garden the stalks will wither; if she sees a baby his skull will crack open.[11]

Speaking of broken skulls, there are numerous taboos relating to death and the deceased. In fact, the mere presence of a corpse causes the members of a tribe to dispose of it as rapidly as possible. Much of the fear of death is due to the dread of ghosts, the ghosts of the departed. Thus, the Navaho Indians not only burn down a house in which someone has died but will avoid the very site for years afterward, believing it is occupied by the

---

7. H. A. Junod, *Life of a South African Tribe*, London, 1927, Vol. I, p. 188.
8. Webster, *Taboo*, p. 212.
9. *Ibid.*, p. 81.
10. E. Thurston, *Ethnographic Notes in Southern India*, Madras, 1907, p. 549.
11. E. W. Smith and A. M. Dale, *The Ila-speaking Peoples of Northern Rhodesia*, London, 1920, Vol. II, p. 10f.

spirit of the dead person.[12] The Tiwi of Melville Island, near Australia, not only refrain from mentioning a dead man's name but any word that has a similar sound. Again, the reason is fear that his ghost will return.[13]

Primitive man's notion that the ghost of the deceased will return is founded on the idea that all things, living and nonliving, have spirits. Upon the death of a living object, its spirit remains in communication with the body in which it was incarnated. This is also the case with man, and herein lies the basis for ancestor worship. Indeed, primitive man believes that his ancestors are forever lurking nearby.

B. Taboos Against Theft and Murder

Not only are primitive man's ancestors hovering in the background; they are actually watching over him. This belief gives him much comfort. For by feeling that his hostile environment is inhabited by spirits upon whom he may depend, he is relieved of some of his apprehension. However, in order to receive their help, he must be on good terms with them.

One way of being in their good graces is to offer them food. And this is where taboos against theft arise. For to steal food which has been placed at the ancestral altar could bring divine punishment. Since not only the tribe as a whole, but each family as well, has its individual ancestor, theft of food offerings or even of family property could incur ancestral displeasure. Subsequently, all theft is outlawed.

The custom of placing the first fruits of the harvest before the altar has indeed been widespread. In the Fiji Islands the ancestral spirit was the first to receive the food

12. Webster, *Taboo*, p. 176.
13. *Ibid.*, pp. 185–86.

of the yam harvest. No one was permitted to eat the yams until the ceremonies pertaining to the food offer had been performed. Moreover, it was believed that if a person stole food from the altar he would be stricken with madness.[14] In the Tonga Islands, yams were presented to the ancestral god just before the crop reached maturity. The offering was made directly to the divine chief, or Tui Tonga, who was allegedly the favored descendant of the god. To forego this ceremony would bring divine vengeance.[15] Among the Thonga, in Africa, no one is allowed to eat any of the new crop until the gods, chief, subchiefs, counselors, headmen and even older brothers have received their share. Should any ordinary tribesmen help himself before the gods and honored mortals had been properly provided, he would be divinely punished.[16]

Another way of being in the gods' good graces is not to commit murder, at least of a kinsman. For since the tribal god is the common ancestor of all the tribesmen, the murder of a kinsman would doubtless incur his wrath. Hence, murder of fellow clansmen is likewise forbidden.

To be sure, if a primitive tribe has been fortunate enough to have lived in perpetual peace with its neighbors, it will condemn all homicide, both within and beyond the tribal boundaries. Thus, the tribes of Central Australia,[17] the Veddahs of Ceylon,[18] and the Eskimo of Greenland[19] condemn the killing of friends and strangers alike.

On the contrary, societies in a frequent state of war condemn homicide among their own members but condone it toward the out-group. Why? Because the out-

---

14. Webster, *Taboo*, p. 342.
15. *Ibid.*, p. 343.
16. Junod, *Life of a South African Tribe.* Vol. I, pp. 394, 404.
17. Sir Baldwin Spencer and F. J. Gillen, *The Native Tribes of Central Australia*, London, 1899, p. 32.
18. Edward Westermarck, *The Origin and Development of the Moral Ideas*, London, 1906, Vol. I, pp. 333–34.
19. F. Nansen, *Eskimo Life*, London, 1893, p. 162.

group appears to be so alien and hostile that even its gods and spirits are of little concern to the in-group. There are countless examples of primitive societies whose members were hardly deterred from, and in fact even encouraged, to attack those in the out-group. The Kafirs of northern India regarded as criminal the slaying of fellow tribesmen, but the murder of strangers didn't disturb them.[20] The Aleuts put to death a person who killed a member of the tribe; one who slew a stranger went free.[21] The Nootka Indians considered the murder of a nonmember to be no more serious than the killing of a dog.[22] The Melanesians looked upon all strangers as enemies meriting death.[23] The Samoans richly rewarded a man who killed an enemy in battle.[24] Among the African Thonga those who slew enemy tribesmen received praise and glory.[25] Among many of the Plains Indians the brave who collected the most scalps was held in the highest esteem.[26]

Thus, so great has been the apprehension of primitive man that he has been frequently incited to acts of cruelty. For the same reason he has observed irrational taboos that pertain to sex and the life cycle as well as the more rational prohibitions which have served to protect life and property, at least within his own circle.

We can readily assume that the taboos which have been upheld in the primitive world existed in prehistoric times. They could then no doubt have been found among Neolithic man. As such, however, they eventually gave rise to the asceticism of later world religions. The taboos relating to sex led at times to the practice of celibacy; those proscribing theft led to restrictions on food intake; those banning murder led to a mistreatment of oneself.

20. Scott-Robertson, *Kafirs of the Hindu Kush*, London, 1896. p. 194.
21. Westermarck, *Origin and Development of Moral Ideas*, p. 332.
22. Sproat. *Scenes and Studies of Savage Life*, p. 152.
23. R. H. Codrington, *Melanesians*, Oxford, 1891, p. 345.
24. H. H. Pritchard, *Polynesian Reminiscences*, London, 1856, p. 57.
25. Junod, *Life of a South African Tribe*, I, p. 447f.
26. Westermarck, *Origin and Development of Moral Ideas*, p. 333.

That is, they encouraged some people to impose even greater limitations on themselves. However, this tendency to live such rigid and austere lives was hardly the occasion in the prehistoric world. Rather, asceticism was a phenomenon of late ancient times, when man's conscience compelled him to atone for crime.

3

Crime and Self-Punishment In The Ancient World

A. The Three Types of Civilized Societies

Journeying from the primitive to the ancient and civilized world would not be as great a step as we may imagine. For among the ancient peoples also, taboo and tradition were at first the order of the day. They too had their taboos of questionable value that related to the life cycle. They too had their more useful prohibitions of theft and homicide, though again these bans were usually limited to the circle of the tribe or state. They, too, had their gods and also their spirits; the former were appealed to, the latter, avoided. These taboos and religious beliefs of early ancient man were the heritage of his primitive ancestors.

In our brief account of primitive societies, we saw that they adhere to tradition and taboo because they feel uneasy in their surroundings. We could even say that those which feel uneasiest adhere most fervently. This rule definitely applied to the ancient peoples also. Those which felt continually menaced by natural circumstances or by neighboring societies were most prone to uphold the rigid mores of their ancestors. Especially those whose neighbors were hostile and, at the same time, formidable felt that they had to follow slavishly the customs and mores handed down to them, even though some of these norms were of questionable value. This was due to their heightened feelings of anxiety, heightened because of their being constantly face to face with peril.

On the other hand, there were societies in the ancient world that felt that they could relax their tension. This being so, they could follow less rigidly the customary modes of conduct. Which of the ancient societies believed they could do this? The answer is those whose neighbors were either friendlier or, if hostile, then not formidable. Shall we say those which either got along better with the other tribes or states and conducted business transactions with them, or else defeated them in battle and lorded it over their countries.

At this point, we may conveniently divide the ancient (and all other civilized) societies into three categories: those which were continually fearful of the surrounding peoples, those which traded with them as well as fought with them occasionally and those which conquered and ruled over them.

The fearful societies were usually newcomers to their respective territories, having migrated from very undesirable locations. The migrations themselves had been hazardous undertakings and had caused the migrants to keep ever closer together. Among them, tribal bonds and blood relationships had been steadfastly maintained, with little regard shown toward those who lived beyond the tribal boundaries. Also, owing to their adverse circumstances, these peoples had been very careful to observe the customary taboos. Alongside such rigid adherence was a deep reverence, coupled with a profound fear of the supernatural, and these attitudes were the very essence of their religion. Tribal solidarity, hostility toward strangers, a close observance of the taboos, and an intense desire to be in divine grace—these were the hallmarks of a migrating people, owing to their dread of the surroundings. Furthermore, their new homes were not such as to allay these fears. Hence, even after reaching their destination, they continued to behave as they did when they were migrating. Accordingly, I shall call these societies *migratory*.

More relaxed than the migratory peoples were those who were able to settle by the sea. This maritime location not only gave the settlers greater protection; it also allowed them to enter into predominantly commercial instead of warlike relations with their neighbors. Naturally, the maintaining of peace in the course of trade made these sea dwellers less tense. Accordingly, they had less need for group solidarity, so that among them tribal affinities gave way to individual considerations. Then too, the act of trading often entailed an exchange of ideas, and in the process of this exchange, taboos and traditions were not adhered to as rigidly as before. Indeed, some of the traditions came to be questioned, particularly by those who were most active in promoting commercial enterprises and were enriched by them. For with the accumulation of wealth, these venturesome individuals acquired self-confidence. Such being the case, they changed the system of government to suit themselves, introduced new forms of writing, or began to doubt the religious beliefs handed down by their forefathers. Some of them even displayed generosity toward the out-group. The attitudes and perspectives of these rich merchants, shipowners and shopmasters—leaders in their societies—were prompted by the exchange of goods and interflow of ideas, in effect, by interaction. Since these societies were influenced more by the process of interaction than by that of migration, I shall call them *interactive*.

These interactive societies, however, were not completely integrated units. For while some of their members had become rich, others had become destitute. The poverty of the latter was due to the change from a rural and tribal to an urban and individualistic economy. These less fortunate individuals, with their added loneliness and frustration, longed for a return to the tribal pattern, through which they could again have a sense of belonging. Accordingly, they established migratory religious cults. Hence, within the very framework of the interactive society, there emerged migratory communities.

As for the third group of societies—those which conquered rather than only traded with or continued to fear the out-group—they, too, had their rich and poor, indeed very rich and very poor. Only among these ancient imperialistic peoples, the upper class came to comprise those who reaped the spoils of war rather than the profits of trade; it was a military aristocracy instead of a commercial plutocracy. At the same time, the lower class included not alone the vanquished, but those among the victors who were impoverished rather than enriched by the imperialism. Here too, the upper class felt it could ignore taboo, and this owing to the self-esteem which followed their successful military exploits. Likewise, the members of the lower class, being destitute, enserfed or enslaved, and without hope of betterment, also joined migratory cults. Hence, the socio-political structure and sentiments of those belonging to the imperialistic societies were determined by their imperialism or expansion. Hence, I shall label these societies *expansive*.

Among many members of the expansive upper class, however, there was a deep feeling of sympathy for the out-group. This feeling was inevitable if the conquerors found it difficult to justify their conquest and if the empire was of long duration. From the sympathy felt for those who were subjugated it was one more step to having feelings of guilt over the misery inflicted. It was these guilt feelings and the need to atone which formed the basis of some of the leading religious creeds—Brahmanism, Buddhism, and Christianity. And in these creeds, the taboos of both real and questionable value were again observed, though in a modified form. Here, they appeared as asceticism.

With this brief introduction, let us now consider first the migratory societies of the ancient world.

B. The Migratory Societies of the Ancient World

Considering first the migratory societies of ancient times, we may assume that all peoples, at the beginning of their history, experienced an age of migration. When the Egyptians made the journey from western Asia to the valley of the Nile, and the Sumerians and Semites traveled from central Asia and Arabia, respectively, to the Tigris-Euphrates Valley, they no doubt passed through a migratory stage. When the Iranians and Indo-Aryans left the wild region of Bactria and found their present homes, and the Greeks and Italians descended from the Alpine foothills to settle on the sunny shores of the Mediterranean, they, too, passed through this stage. So did the Chinese, upon reaching the Yellow River, also the Japanese upon arriving in their five scenic islands. This means that all of these peoples had at one time the anxieties and prohibitions associated with that particular age.

However, of all the ancient peoples, there were three who looked upon their neighbors with greater apprehension than did any of the others. These three peoples lived in deep fear of the societies beyond, and even among themselves there was mutual antagonism and distrust. Who were these especially apprehensive folk? They were the Hebrews, the Greeks, and the Italians.

From the time of their origin, the Hebrews were the perfect example of a migrating or migratory society. In the Pentateuch we read that the patriarch Abraham and his family migrated from Ur, in Mesopotamia, to Canaan, in Palestine. Not much later, when a famine descended upon the land of Canaan, his progeny moved to Egypt.

There they remained, it is said, for four hundred years, until forced to flee by the rise of a hostile dynasty in that country.

There can be little question that the Hebrews held fast to the taboos so common among primitive folk. This they did long after their resettlement in Palestine. In the Pentateuch, which was written many centuries after the fall of Jericho, there were set forth a number of the familiar bans, familiar in that they related to the life cycle. For example, a woman, having given birth to a child, was considered unclean, and anything she touched was likewise believed to be contaminated. Also regarded as impure were the fact of menstruation and the act of intercourse. Needless to say, all women undergoing these experiences and all men having had contact with them had to bathe. Even then either were considered as being clean until sundown. In the Pentateuch we read:

"The woman also with whom man shall lie with seeds of copulation, they shall both bathe themselves in water and be unclean until the even.

"And anything that she lieth upon in her separation shall be unclean; everything also that she sitteth upon shall be unclean.

"And if any man lie with her at all, and her flowers be upon him, he shall be unclean seven days, and all the bed whereupon he lieth shall be unclean."[1]

About death and the deceased, too, the Hebrews had the familiar apprehensions. Not only were corpses considered to be contaminating, but all burial grounds were located at some distance from the towns.[2]

Finally, there were restrictions as to which foods could be eaten. Generally, fruits, vegetables and grain were consumed at mealtime. But then only the flesh of beasts which

1. Leviticus 15:18, 20, 24.
2. John Kitto, *Palestine from the Patriarchal Age to the Present Time*, London, 1920, p. 89.

grazed and had segmented hoofs, or of fish which had scales and fins, were permitted for repast. Other meat and seafood were from animals which were regarded as strange or unnatural and therefore harmful.[3]

Quite possibly, the Hebrews had come to believe that these foods were prohibited by their gods. At the time of their settlement in Egypt, each of the Hebrew tribes had as its chief deity a god of fertility from whom the group received its name. Thus, the tribe of Gad worshiped the god Gad, the tribe of Asher revered the goddess Ashera, and so on.[4] Since the tribal gods and goddesses were agricultural deities, they could easily be angered by any infraction of their alleged laws pertaining to food.

In the thirteenth century B.C., and after the Hebrews began to experience persecution in Egypt, the different tribes came to worship one God, Yahweh. Originally, Yahweh was the god of fertility among the non-Hebrew tribe of Kenites, but it was from this tribe that the prophet Moses had taken a wife. With the subsequent hardships which the Hebrews faced when again in the desert, Yahweh became a deity who had no special locale, nor was he a mere nature god. Rather than being identified with a certain place, he was identified with all places; instead of being an agricultural, solar, or sky god, he became a universal God. For the Hebrews needed a god who was independent of any single locality or natural force. Only a god who was above such limitations could give the Hebrews the comforts and consolation which they so sorely required in the desert wilderness, where they were surrounded by ever-watchful enemies.

With the resettlement in the land of Canaan and the establishment of the Jewish state, the authority and divinity of the one god were conceived as upholding the various Hebrew customs and sanctions. To violate one of them

---

3. Kitto, *Palestine*, p. 61.
4. G. A. Barton, *The Religions of the World*, Chicago, 1919, pp. 60–61.

was to incur his wrath and bring punishment. If the Jewish state failed to observe the particular mores and the
Mosaic laws, the society in its entirety would be punished.
Such was the agreement set forth in the covenant. In this
famous document the Hebrews agreed to abide by their
laws and mores, if they wished to continue receiving divine protection. On the other hand, any violation of this
sacred pact could bring destruction to the entire country.
Thus, the Hebrew god appeared as a stern father, who frequently aroused fear. Yet this characteristic of Judaism
was but a reflection of the continued state of tension.

Apprehension over strangers or foreigners only strengthens in-group feeling, and this was the case with the Hebrews. They were continually conscious, indeed too conscious, of a distinction between their society and others,
between themselves and the out-group. Consequently, in
time of war they, like other neighboring migratory societies—the Philistines, Amorites, and Assyrians—were
ruthless toward those they subdued. Especially toward
idolatrous people did they show little mercy, since toward
them they could find religious sanction for their policy
of near extermination.[5] But the real basis of this policy
was a wariness born of fear.

In their taboos, religious beliefs, and attitudes toward
foreigners the Hebrews resembled the Greeks of Homeric
times (1200-900 b.c.). For like the Hebrew tribes the
Greek clans were also wary and apprehensive. They, too,
had migrated to a new homeland—the Greek peninsula—
and having settled there, established city-states. Moreover,
each Greek community was well aware that neither the
scenic mountains, in its new homeland, nor even the walls
of its city could guarantee sufficient protection against
enemies. Hence, there was continued tension within these
walls.

One evidence of this tension was a certain wariness of

5. Westermarck, *Origin and Development of Moral Ideas,* p. 339.

the physical atmosphere. For the Greeks believed in the existence of tiny demons, or *keres*. The *keres* were always trying to enter their bodies and do them harm. Once inside a person's body, they caused him to become ill and, if sufficiently strong, could bring about his death. To have contact with a sick person meant exposure to the *keres* and contraction of the same disease; to approach a dead person was certainly to risk illness or even loss of life.[6] Whenever a Greek left a house where there was a corpse, he took water from a vessel at the door and sprinkled his body with it, his purpose being to protect himself from the *keres* which had overcome the dead man.[7]

The obsession with the *keres* extended to still other phases of Greek life. Birth, sexual intercourse and childbirth were believed to render a person particularly susceptible to these demons. Therefore, anyone having experienced these acts had to undergo a purification ceremony.[8] In fact, at certain intervals throughout the year, camps, temples, meeting places, and even entire cities were "purified" through the use of water, smoke, or fire, so as to avoid widespread contamination and plague.[9]

Fire was considered to be not only purifying but, in some instances, sacred. Every Greek household had its sacred fire, which embodied the spirit of Hestia, goddess of the hearth. This fire was transmitted from mother to daughter. When a young wife was escorted to the house of her husband, her mother led the way, carrying a torch that had been lit from her hearth. With this torch she lighted a new fire in the house of her son-in-law.[10] Every courtyard also had its sacred flames, which represented Zeus Herkeios (Zeus of the Garth) and were passed on

---

6. J. E. Harrison, *Prolegomena to the Study of Greek Religion,* Cambridge, 1922, p. 167.
7. M. Nillson, *History of Greek Religion,* Oxford, 1925, pp. 82–83.
8. Harrison, *Prolegomena . . . ,* p. 171.
9. Fustel de Coulanges, *The Ancient City,* Boston, 1873, pp. 213–14.
10. T. Zielinski, *The Religion of Ancient Greece,* Oxford, 1926, p. 91.

from father to son. It was from the altar of Zeus Herkeios that the head of the house took a burning brand, dipped it into a pail of water, and with it sprinkled the members of the family. By means of this ritual the family members were freed from impurity and also spiritually united.[11] Aside from Hestia and Zeus Herkeios there were ancestral spirits which kept watch over the household. Before the deities and spirits alike purity of behavior had to be maintained. Moreover, even beyond the hearth and the homestead adultery was strictly prohibited, since a child born out of wedlock could not take part in the ceremonies.[12]

Just as each household had its altars to Hestia and Zeus Herkeios so did each community of clans, or city, have its temples to Hestia; Zeus the sky god and Apollo the sun god. Just as the family members gathered at the altar to seek guidance so did they, as citizens of their city, frequent the temples to seek advice. Such advice was given through the utterings, or "oracles," of the priestesses believed to be in communion with the god. The most famous oracles were in a particular city; those of Zeus were at Dodona, those of Apollo at Delphi. Of course, in return for guidance, counsel, and protection the Greeks offered food and gifts.

The concern over purity, adoration of household deities, and frequent seeking of counsel reflected a fear of what lay beyond, or what was unfamiliar. And such apprehension only strengthened in-group sentiment. This, in turn, influenced the Greek attitude toward foreigners. Persons from beyond the city walls had no legal rights and received little protection from murder and theft, although such offenses were not too common, because of fear of angry ghosts.[13] However, war in the Homeric age was a cruel

---

11. *Ibid.*, p. 93.
12. Coulanges, *The Ancient City*, pp. 125–26.
13. J. G. Frazer, *The Fear of the Dead in Primitive Religion*, London, 1933, Vol. I, p. 188.

undertaking. The fall of a city was followed by the extermination of the men and enslavement of the women and children. When the Greeks, having laid siege to Troy, finally entered the city, they put all the men to the sword and carried the women and children into captivity. Like the Hebrews, the Greeks in the migratory age felt little remorse for these actions, as they, too, lived in a state of perpetual tension.

The uneasiness that prevailed in the Hebrew and Greek communities also existed in the Italian, for the inhabitants of Italy lived amid similar circumstances. In Italy, as in Greece and Palestine, warfare was almost a common occurrence. From the slopes of the Apennines one could too often view the spectacle of a battle between arrays of soldiers, their helmets, breast plates, and shields glittering in the sunlight, while their javelins and short swords were shedding blood on the otherwise green fields.

As we know, of all the Italian societies it was the Roman which finally obtained mastery of the peninsula. But prior to their military achievement, the Romans had an even better reason than did the early Hebrews, Athenians, and Spartans to be wary of those who lived beyond their city walls. For in 390 B.C. the Gauls, having laid waste the Plains of Latium, scaled the Roman walls and pillaged the city. "The Gauls came, murdered all they met with, plundered whatever property they found, and at length set the city on fire on all sides, before the eyes of the Roman garrison in the Capitol."[14] The Romans never forgot this episode. And the memory of it, together with their general apprehension, influenced their religious and social outlook.

The Romans also were obsessed with the need for purity. They too worried about being infected by such supposedly impure acts as sexual intercourse, childbirth, and burial

---

14. T. Mommsen, *History of Rome*, London, 1881, Vol. I, p. 342.

of the dead.[15] They likewise insisted upon the performance
of purification ceremonies by those who experienced such
acts.[16] These rites were performed also before family altars.

Like the Greeks, the Romans had their sacred fires. Each
family had its maternal fire, which blazed before the altar
of Vesta (Hestia), and paternal fire that represented
Genius, the guardian spirit of the household. Before both,
elaborate sacrifices were made and allegedly immoral acts
forbidden.[17] Within a special temple erected for the city
there was an altar to Vesta, before which the priestesses
known as vestal virgins kept the sacred fire constantly
burning. Were the fire to go out, destruction would rain
on the city![18] Beyond the boundaries of the city, danger
was supposed to lurk; guarding them was the task of Janus,
god of the gate. To be sure, the Romans also had their
war, harvest, and sky deities—Mars, Ceres, Saturn, and
Jupiter; but the worship of Vesta and Janus, the high
regard for the sacred fire, and fear of the beyond were
especially characteristic of a migratory people.

A third indication that the Romans were migratory was
their belief that the will of the gods could be understood
by means of signs. For just as the Greeks had their oracles,
so did the Romans have their portents and omens. For their
interpretation they consulted the priests known as augurs.
The advice of the augurs was sought before any important
business was transacted. Even questions concerning war
and peace awaited the counsel of the augurs, so concerned
were the Romans about possible misfortune.

The reference to war and peace brings us once more to
the subject of Rome's relations with her neighbors. In
the conduct of war it was again a case of anxiety having
induced a measure of cruelty. When the Romans, from

15. Frazer, *Fear of the Dead* . . . , p. 62.
16. Coulanges, *The Ancient City*, p. 126.
17. *Ibid.*, p. 127.
18. *Ibid.*, pp. 194–95.

326 to 304 B.C., waged war with the Samnites, a rival Italian society, they did their share of ravaging and plundering. But particularly toward their old enemies, the Gauls, did they show little mercy. In the conflict waged against the Etruscans and their Gallic allies, from 285 to 282 B.C., a Roman contingent had been attacked by the Senones, a Gallic tribe, whereupon "the consul Publius Cornelius Dolabella advanced with a strong army into their (Senone) territory; all that were not put to the sword were driven from the land; and the tribe was erased from the list of the Italian nations."[19] The Romans hardly felt guilty over this massacre, since the Gauls were not only an out-group but, traditionally, a formidable one.

In effect, the early Romans, other Italians, Greeks, and Hebrews had all the characteristics of migrating peoples. They were wary of situations which they didn't understand, a wariness born of intertribal or international conflict. Confronted with hostile environments, they were obsessed with fears of contamination. Hence, they observed taboos which related to the life cycle and depended upon their deities and spirits to protect them from both impurity and assaults from enemies. Living in fear of the beyond, their communities maintained in-group feeling; with such strong solidarity, they continued to be hostile to the outside world.

A final word about their group solidarity. Within the tribe or city-state, each member felt a common affinity with a god, or with a patron deity. Moreover, among the members themselves there was usually little difference with respect to wealth or social rank. Perhaps the only exception to this rule was in Rome, where there was a division between the patricians (older families) and plebians (newcomers), but this difference was eventually resolved. In the Greek or Italian community and Hebrew

---

19. Mommsen, *History of Rome*, p. 402.

nation, the leaders of clans or tribes, respectively, were highly influential. The king of the Hebrews or of the Greek or Italian city-state had to consult with tribal chieftains or heads of clans before making a move. This situation, of course, strengthened the traditions and conservatism of the migratory society, and withal its hostility to the outside.

If, however, the society itself migrated to the coast and changed to a maritime economy, its traditional heads faced ouster by a rising commercial class. On this occasion, the migratory societal organization became interactive.

C. The Interactive Societies of the Ancient World

Earlier I stated that the interactive societies showed less inner tension than the migratory. How was this lesser degree of tension manifested? It was seen in their skepticism toward the ideas handed down to them from the migratory age. It was further indicated in their greater tolerance of strangers. In these trading societies the wealthy urban citizens questioned the traditional forms of government and religion inherited from the migratory age. As a result, the interactive society was frequently the scene of political change and lively philosophic speculation. It was likewise the scene of a slightly friendlier attitude toward the out-group.

Where, in ancient times, could we find interactive societies? We could find them among the Phoenicians and Ionic Greeks. Both of these peoples were active traders; both saw the growth of merchant classes which overthrew aristocratic migratory regimes. Both had within their communities numerous individuals who looked with skepticism on the teachings of priests and elders and introduced thought systems of their own.

The earliest of the ancient societies to break with the

past were the Phoenician cities of Tyre and Sidon. In these communities the trading classes seized control of the government and exercised power through elected assemblies. Whereas in Sidon the assembly, when enacting legislation, virtually ignored the king, in Tyre it actually replaced him.

However, this was not their only break with tradition. Another, and one of far-reaching consequence, was their introduction of the phonetic alphabet. We know that for centuries the peoples of the Near East were instructed by their priests in the use of the pictorial or symbolic alphabet. This holds true for the Egyptians, with their hieroglyphics, and the Sumerians and Semitic Babylonians, with their cuneiform writing. During these centuries the Phoenicians were no exception. Being Semitic, they, too, had used the cuneiform system. But when they adopted the phonetics, they defied both their own priests and the Babylonian rulers. This adoption helped them to become the businessmen and traders they were.

The break with the past, which began in Phoenicia, was carried to greater lengths in Ionic Greece. Why Ionic, instead of Doric or Aeolian Greece? Because it was the Ionic cities which became flourishing commercial centers. The liveliest of these communities were Miletus, Ephesus, and Athens; all were pioneers in defying convention. This they did with regard to politics, philology, and philosophy.

Miletus and Ephesus were in an excellent position to give and receive commodities and ideas alike. Located on the coast of Asia Minor, with Egypt, Assyria, and Babylonia to the south, Persia to the east, and mainland Greece to the west, they were veritable emporias for both trade and knowledge. They were as truly interactive, if not more so, as Tyre and Sidon.

Like the Phoenicians, they too established governments in which their shipowners, traders, and workshop masters had the upper hand. They, too, made vast improvements in their methods of communication. After learning the Phoenician alphabet, they added the vowel sounds, thus rendering it even more suitable for conducting business.

This newly revised alphabet proved of vital importance in other ways. It led to attempts to explain the universe in a different way, and this, in turn, meant a further questioning of the beliefs upheld by priests and elders. Such inquiry marked the birth of Western philosophy.

Significantly, the first philosopher, Thales of Miletus, (c. 624-545 B.C.), was from a family of Phoenician merchants, the very people whose tendency was to doubt. His merchant-class origin may also have led him to conceive of water as the source of all things. Be that as it may, in contending that everything originates from water he helped to undermine the belief that events are caused by the whims of the gods.

In partly destroying this notion Thales was assisted by two other philosophers of the same city and one from nearby Ephesus. They were Anaximander (611-547 B.C.), who contended that a "balance of elements" is primary; Anaximines (c. 600 B.C.), who considered air to be the basic substance; and Heraclitus (540-475 B.C.), who maintained that fire is the fundamental element and transforms into the others. With these speculations as to the nature and possible origin of the universe, the traditional theology came to be questioned.

Philosophic systems have a tendency to be highly influential. The virtual materialism and skepticism, current in Miletus and Ephesus, found their way to the flourishing city-state of Athens. There, in the fifth century B.C., long after the end of the Homeric age, they reached their apex. For in no other community was interaction so evident. The spectacle along the Attican coast was one of numerous triremes plying back and forth with their various cargoes, while the Athenian wharfs and warehouses were the scene of constant bustle. The workshops were perpetually humming with activity, turning out the tripods, wine cups, and vases for which Greece became famous. The agora was, day by day, crowded with men discussing business and listening to heated debates and fiery oratory.

It was such debating and oratory that contributed to the political changes that transpired in Athens, during the sixth and fifth centuries. Through a series of revolutions, the Athenian trading classes had overthrown the aristocratic Council of Areopagus and established the Ekklesia, or assembly, as the principal governing body. With their influence in the Ekklesia, the merchants and shipowners of Athens could conduct the affairs of state pretty much to suit themselves.

Amid such an atmosphere of political change, philosophic speculation was furthered. Empedocles (c. 490-430 B.C.) conceived of the world as being made from earth, air, fire, and water; Anaxagoras (c. 500-428 B.C.) saw these four elements as being easily transformed into one another. Finally, Leucippus (fifth century B.C.) and Democritus (c. 470-380 B.C.) regarded them as being divisible into tiny atoms, those minute bodies which, through their combination, had formed the universe. With this hypothesis, Leucippus and Democritus all but denied the role played by the gods in creating natural forces.

The growth of trade and industry and the questioning of tradition and authority were among the more favorable aspects of Athenian life. For there was another and more ominous phase, which could be found not only in Greece but in any country where the land was not especially fertile. This was the impoverishment of the majority of small farmers. How had these modest country dwellers become so poor? For one thing, they understood little about crop rotation and fertilization, so that their soil gradually became exhausted.[20] For another, they insisted upon dividing their property among their heirs, until the

20. G. Glotz, *Ancient Greece at Work,* New York, 1926, p. 64.

farms were too small to support the occupants.[21] For still another, every time there was war between the cities, crops were ravaged and livestock destroyed.

Being destitute, these small proprietors were compelled to borrow from wealthy neighbors. But this posed great difficulties. True, during the migratory age, when in-group feelings were strong, a more fortunate landowner would have been under moral obligation to assist a struggling kinsman. But in the interactive period the wealthy sold their surpluses only for a profit. This meant that money or goods loaned to a neighbor brought with it a heavy charge of interest. Most of the debtor farmers were unable to pay back their loans. This being the case, they were forced to mortgage their farms and, on some occasions, themselves. In effect, a number of them became the slaves of their creditors.[22]

As for the wealthy landowners—the older nobility and the rich traders and shipowners who had purchased estates —they were fortunate indeed. Only they had the means with which to convert their grain farms to grape or olive cultivation, for which the Greek soil was more suited. Only they could divide their holdings and yet be assured that their heirs would still be in comfortable circumstances. Only they were able to protect their property from pillagers in time of war. As time elapsed the gulf between the rich and the poor became ever wider. Thus, it is hardly surprising that alongside the aristocracy and plutocracy the poorer people came to feel that they were not only impoverished persons but outcasts.

Being in such a state of mind, the poorer classes found the Olympian religion to be too formal and aristocratic. After all, the nobles looked upon themselves as the "sons of Zeus," and the temples and altars came to have about

---

21. *Ibid.,* p. 98.
22. Glotz, *Ancient Greece* . . . , pp. 80–81.

them an air of stateliness.[23] On the other hand, the propertyless and under privileged did not, or could not, welcome the skepticism of the trading classes, craftsmen as well as merchants. What they needed was a religion which would bring them into close contact with a new and vital supernatural power. What they fervently desired was to worship a god or goddess whose very being they could share.[24] It was here that the mysteries made their appearance.

The mysteries actually originated in the desolate regions of Thrace and Phrygia, in Asia Minor, where the inhabitants were hardly affected by civilization. Yet, after being transplanted to mainland Greece, they were on fertile soil. Among the many mystery cults which flourished, the Eleusinian and the Orphic were the most popular. The devotees of both worshiped the Chthonian, or earthly, as contrasted with the Olympian, or heavenly, deities. The Eleusinians went through a series of prescribed nocturnal rituals, which involved much emotional behavior. Their purpose was the adoration of Demeter, the Aegean earth goddess, and her daughter, Persephone, who they believed would watch over their souls during the dark and endless journey through Hades.[25] The Orphists displayed even more intense emotional outbursts, as they were imitating Orpheus, the child of the moon and the nine muses. Their noctural ceremonies were accompanied by drinking and had as their object of worship Dionysius, the god of wine and vitality. By partaking of wine and engaging in rites considered as symbolic of life itself, the Orphists believed that they could obtain immortality.[26]

It is significant that at these rituals the worshipers prayed for abundance and also for wisdom and the will to

23. *Ibid.*, p. 73.
24. G. Thompson, *Aeschylus and Athens*, London, 1941, pp. 151, 159.
25. Harrison, *Prolegomena* . . . , pp. 539–57.
26. *Ibid.*, pp. 473–77.

remain chaste. It is equally significant that no discrimination was made among the devotees with respect to either wealth or nobility of birth. In effect, it could be said that the mysteries reflected the desire on the part of many persons living in the interactive period of Greek history to return to the earlier migratory period. In fact, these many discontented individuals wished to revert to the very earliest centuries of the migratory age. For this was before a hereditary aristocracy had even developed and in-group feeling was very potent.

The mysteries, in turn, had a direct bearing on philosophic thought. Indeed, one of the philosophers founded a mystery society himself. This was Pythagoras (582-493 B.C.), the son of a gem maker and an immigrant from the island of Samos to southern Italy. It was in the south of Italy (Magna Graecia) that Pythagoras established his society and philosophic creed. In contrast to the Milesian, Ephesian, and Athenian philosophers, Pythagoras was an idealist. He regarded as unreal the world of matter and change; he even considered such a world to be harmful and as leading men toward vice and corruption. Rather, he believed that only the soul, allegedly the one constant factor in man, was beneficial. The soul, he asserted, desires nothing more than to escape from the sensory world of evil and seek haven in the unseen realm of good. This it does by means of transmigration.

Pythagoras was not the only philosopher to be influenced by the popular cults. Others were Xenophanes (sixth century B.C.), also an immigrant to Italy; his pupil, Parmenides (c. 500 B.C.), and the latter's student, Zeno (fifth century B.C.). Together, they stated that the only reality in the universe is being, a changeless and eternal substance; together, they held all sensory impressions to be illusory. Their school was located in the city of Elea, a remote corner of the Greek world, a place far removed from the thriving trade centers of the Aegean. Here, idealistically minded men of thought could preserve the sanctity of their souls and seek a supernatural power that would protect them from an indifferent and competitive social order.

Eventually, the mysteries influenced the intellectual life of Athens herself. Their spirit could be seen in the Greek tragic drama, a performance which had its very origin in the Dionysian festivals. These tragedies were portrayals of human misconduct and of the misery which followed. In the plays of Aeschylus (525-426 B.C.), Sophocles (496-405 B.C.) and Euripides (480-406 B.C.) man has violated taboos, committed sins and thereby offended the gods; for so doing he has been punished. Indeed, the dramas appeared to warn their audience that the only way to preserve their souls is to avoid the pitfalls of immorality. This theme was stressed particularly by Aeschylus and Sophocles.

With Euripides, however, there was a certain parting of the ways. For while speaking of divine wrath and punishment, he also rebelled against the Olympian pantheon. His revolt was not sparked by Orphist doctrine, since the mysteries, although puritanic, were not revolutionary movements. Rather, he was stirred by different currents. As a young man he was taught by Anaxagoras, whose skepticism he came to share.[27] Not much later Euripides was inspired by the humanitarian teachings of Protagoras (480-410 B.C.), who maintained that "man is the measure of all things."[28] Both Anaxagoras and Protagoras were true spokesmen of an interactive age, and their ideas bore fruit in the works of this eminent dramatist. In *The Children of Heracles*, Euripides reprimanded the gods for demanding a human sacrifice as the price of a military victory; in *The Suppliants*, he stood strongly in favor of written laws to protect all citizens. In *The Trojan Women*,

27. Gilbert Murray, *Euripides and His Age*, New York, 1913, p. 50.
28. *Ibid.*, p. 54.

Euripides expressed deep sympathy for a foreign society which had been vanquished by his fellow Greeks. Here he portrays vividly the grief of the Trojan Queen, Hecuba, at the fall of her city:

> Who am I that I sit here at the Greek King's door
> ⸴Yea, in the dust of it? A slave that men drive before,
> A woman that hath no home, weeping alone for her dead
> A low and bruised head and the glory struck therefrom.[29]

Euripides' sense of compassion had come about only through a broadening of understanding beyond the narrow limits of the city-state. Interaction had rendered this possible.

While Euripides was the loftiest figure of interaction, Socrates (469–399 B.C.) was the noblest individual of the migratory reaction. For Socrates was interested in matters of the soul and salvation. In his quest for truth, Socrates identified the true with the ethical and the false with what he thought to be vulgar and mundane. But in searching for the ethical he criticized the Olympian religion for placing too little stress on this quality. For this he was told to recant or make the supreme sacrifice. Even an interactive society could at times be intolerant.

The conflict between interactive and migratory sentiment, between realism and idealism, continued well into the next century, when Plato (427–347 B.C.) and Aristotle 384–322 B.C.) took opposite sides. Plato, the idealist, was the herald for reaction; Aristotle, a realist, the flag-bearer for progress.

At the time that he formulated his philosophy, Plato was a thoroughly embittered man. Having experienced the death of his teacher, Socrates, and having lived through the Peloponnesian War (434–404 B.C.), he became disillusioned with life as he found it. He therefore devised a system of philosophy in which all sensory impressions

---

29. Euripides, *The Trojan Women*, trans. G. Murray, London, 1919, p. 18.

were conceived as mere shadows of the one Idea. He also advocated a return to the Homeric age, and in his *Laws* and *Republic* he urged the Greeks to uphold tradition and adhere to the customs of their ancestors.

Plato's philosophy ran into sharp criticism from his student, Aristotle. This was inevitable, since Aristotle lived at a different time. His was an age that saw the revival of Athenian prosperity, though under foreign rule. Aristotle's studies and experiences in the revived city made him the true spokesman of an interactive epoch. Whereas Plato believed in respecting the founding fathers of the Greek city-states, Aristotle had grave doubts about their wisdom and about the laws which they devised. He comments:

"The remains of the ancient laws which have come down to us are quite absurd; for example, at Cumae there is a law about murder, to the effect that if the accuser produce a certain number of witnesses from among his own kinsmen, the accused shall be held guilty. Again men in general desire the good and not merely what their fathers had. But the primeval inhabitants, whether they were born of the earth or were the survivors of some destruction, may be supposed to have been no better than ordinary or even foolish people among ourselves . . . and it would be ridiculous to rest contented with their notions."[30]

Thus to Aristotle tradition was of little value unless it served the needs of the times. Since he regarded the laws and customs of the remote past as being outdated, he was opposed to a restoration of the Homeric age. Rather, he welcomed the new Hellenistic era begun by his contemporary, Alexander the Great, though it was one of imperialistic expansion. With expansion, however, new trends were set in motion.

---

30. *Politics*, trans. B. Jowett. from *The Oxford Translation of Aristotle*, ed. W. D. Ross, Oxford, 1921, Bk. II, Ch. 8.

D. The Expansive Societies of the Ancient World

The reference to the Hellenistic empire brings us to the third group of societies—the *expansive*. But before discussing them in detail, let us review very briefly what was said concerning the migratory and interactive tribes and states of ancient times.

In Section B I maintained that all societies were at one time migratory and lived in constant fear of their surroundings. As such, they observed taboos and adhered closely to tradition. Adherence to tradition only strengthened in-group feeling and hostility toward the out-group. Hence, in time of war they were usually quite ruthless toward those whom they subdued. For examples of migratory societies I selected the Hebrews, Homeric Greeks, and early Romans, since it is they about whom we know most.

In Section C I stated that two of the ancient societies—the Phoenicians and later Ionic Greeks—emerged from their migratory past and became interactive. These peoples continued to observe taboos, but, in other respects, they broke with their migratory past. Their trading classes ousted the kings and aristocratic councils and in their place set up elected assemblies. Their scholars and writers discarded some of the older religious beliefs and looked to philosophy for an explanation of the universe. Alongside these innovations in-group feeling declined slightly, and among a small minority there was friendly feeling toward the out-group.

Considering, at present, the expansive societies—the Assyrians, Babylonians, Egyptians, Hittites, Iranians, Indo-Aryans, Chinese, Japanese, Macedonians, and later Romans —we may note that they also discarded some of their migratory heritage. They, too, changed their form of government, except that their kings and nobles became far more powerful instead of less so; monarchy and aristocracy could best serve the needs of imperialism. Their upper classes likewise discarded the older religions for newer ones blended with philosophy. Indeed, in certain societies the philosophic religions reflected the feelings of the conquerers toward their conquests.

Some societies retained the in-group mentality even after their expansion; hence, they didn't suffer any pangs of conscience over having stolen from or killed members of the out-group. But others, and especially their nobles and rich merchants, began to identify with themselves the people of the countries they subjugated. In so doing their outlook changed. Such persons, in high status, who began to understand only too well the plight of their victims, had feelings of guilt. Having such feelings, they sought to overcome them. How? They did so by renouncing the very manner of living for which their conquests had been undertaken. They forsook material values and sought the life of the spirit. A number of them even went beyond the ordinary taboos which were upheld on matters of sex and practiced celibacy. In effect, they became ascetic and otherworldly. In doing so they were making retribution for crimes committed against others.

Which of the expansive societies were affected the most by pangs of conscience and which the least? Those which felt that they had to conquer in order to protect themselves were not too disturbed by their actions; neither were those whose imperialistic eras were too brief to allow time for reflection. On the contrary, those which plundered, pillaged, and subjugated others for mere profit, or whose imperialistic eras were extended, eventually felt most uneasy. Also, the imperialistic societies whose treatment of their fallen foes was mild had less cause for remorse than did those who were ruthless.

A classic example of a people who seemed to have few misgivings over the manner in which they treated others were the Assyrians. Indeed, the Assyrian kings even boasted of the cruelties they committed. Tiglath-pileser III (744-727 B.C.) compelled 30,000 Hebrews to leave their cities and settled them in the provinces of his empire.[31] Sennacherib (704-681 B.C.) wrote about how he drove 200,000 people, together with their livestock, out of forty-six cities and forced them to live in the more remote corners of his realm.[32] But the greatest cruelties were those of Ashurnasirpal II (883-859 B.C.). This extremely sadistic monarch boasted of the way in which he punished a group of Assyrians who revolted against him. He had the principal leaders of the rebellion impaled; the lesser ones he had decapitated, and their skins and limbs publicly displayed, perhaps as a warning to those who might contemplate revolt in the future.[33]

Significantly, Ashurnasirpal II was one of the earliest of the Assyrian monarchs, but why is this fact significant? Because it was during his reign that the Assyrians, easily exposed to invasion from hostile tribes or nations, felt that they either had to subdue or be subjugated. Hence, such ruthlessness on his part appeared to meet with the tacit approval of his Assyrian subjects; at least there isn't any record of there having been a protest against it. It was this state of tension which prompted the later kings to be almost as merciless and their kinsmen to support such ruthless policies. Throughout the two centuries that their empire endured, the Assyrians retained a completely in-group mentality.

Another society which was almost as cruel and had almost as little regret over its cruelty as the early Babylonian, or Amorite. I say almost as cruel, because while the Amorite rulers were not as sadistic as the Assyrian, they did humiliate the people whom they subjugated. This is indicated in the famous Code of Hammurabi (c.

---

31. J. Finnegan, *Light from the Ancient Past*, Princeton. 1959, p. 207.
32. *Ibid..* p. 212.
33. *Ibid.,* p. 203.

1955-1913 B.C.) . In this earliest of law codes, Hammurabi
arranged for his kinsmen, the Amorites, to be treated as a
privileged caste. Below them came the Sumerians, while
at the very base of the social pyramid were the Elamites,
a people whom he reduced almost to slavery.

As ruthless as the early Babylonians of Hammurabi's
day were the late Babylonians of Nebuchadnezzar's (604-
561 B.C.) . His policy of uprooting an entire nation from
its home was notorious and is mentioned in any text on
ancient history. Again, no apparent word of protest came
from any of the king's subjects. Why did the Babylonians
seem to acquiesce in the mistreatment of others? Simply
because their country, too, was constantly exposed to danger from invasion, a situation which gave them little cause
to regret their actions. Then too, their empires were short-
lived.

From Babylonia we travel to Egypt, where there was
less danger of attack from the outside; there, also, dynasties
were of greater duration, and kingdoms or empires lasted
longer. For Egypt, too, was the scene of imperialism, and
as early as 3500 B.C. It was then that the Kingdom of the
Upper Nile conquered the fertile Delta region and thus
began the period of the Old Kingdom (3500-2160 B.C.) .

True, the pharaohs of the Old Kingdom were cruel.
They compelled whole armies of fellahin (peasants) to
work under the hot sun and the lash erecting pyramids.
But because Egypt was less exposed to invasion, they did
not discriminate among their subjects. Such forced labor
was demanded of virtually all the inhabitants of their
realm, from the Upper as well as from the Lower Nile.
The only classes exempt were the nobles and scribes, the
former because of their social rank, the latter, due to their
ability to have mastered the difficult hieroglyphics. While
the nobles were appointed as nomarchs (governors) and
local magistrates, the scribes were assigned to assist them
in the work of administration.

In the twenty-seventh century B.C. some of the nomarchs showed concern as to whether, during their administrations, they had treated fairly the people living under their jurisdiction. Prior to this time the governors had worried only about having been kind to their own families and near relatives. Had they been unkind to them, they believed they would be punished by their ancestral or even nature gods. But from this century, they began to remind their gods that they had also behaved justly to those who lived within their respective nomarchies. One such nomarch addressed the gods as follows:

"I gave bread to all the hungry of Cerastes Mountain; I clothed him who was naked therein . . . I never oppressed [anyone] in possession of his property, so that he complained of it to the god of my city."[34]

No doubt, many of those residing in this governor's nomarchy were descendants of the conquered peoples; yet, such pledges became increasingly common as time went on.

The Old Kingdom was succeeded by the more feudalistic Middle Kingdom (2160-1580 B.C.). But even though it was feudalistic, the Middle Kingdom experienced moral growth. Not only the nomarchs but pharaoh himself gave such assurances to the gods, particularly to the sun god, Ra, of whom he was regarded as the appointed ruler. Many of the pharaohs, anxious to enter the next world after death, sought to remind Ra that they, likewise, had been kind to widows and orphans and never robbed anyone, rich or poor. Many of them went to great length to describe how considerate they had been of the peasant. Actually, the peasant continued to be poor and severely exploited, but at least a social conscience was slowly developing.

An interesting work of literature, which was popular at the time—that is, among those who could read—was the

34. Quoted from J. H. Breasted, *The Dawn of Conscience*, New York, 1934, p. 26.

"Tale of the Eloquent Peasant." The story opens with a peasant being swindled by a minor official. He lodges complaints with the latter's superior and the local nomarch. Both are moved to such pity that the minor magistrate is compelled to make good the peasant's loss. No doubt, the sentiment expressed in this work was frequently shared by pharaoh and the more humane among the nobility.

The Middle Kingdom came to an end when the Hyksos, an Asian people, invaded Egypt. In fact, with this episode, Egypt experienced her first real foreign invasion. The event left its mark on Egyptian history. For largely because of it, the conscience which was slowly developing along the banks of the Nile was never aroused when it came to dealing with peoples of other lands. During the succeeding period of the New Kingdom, the Egyptians themselves embarked upon an era of expansion into Asia. Under such ambitious pharaohs as Thutmose III (1501-1447 B.C.) and Ramses II (1292-1225 B.C.), they pillaged and conquered Palestine and Syria. But they had little regret for having undertaken such imperialistic ventures.

For the development of a feeling of moral obligation toward neighboring countries, we must turn to the Hittites. A number of the Hittite kings had feelings of guilt after having committed acts of aggression against foreign rulers. For example, in the late thirteenth century B.C., King Muwatallish made an unwarranted attack upon the realm of Ramses II. Shortly afterward, the Hittites experienced a devastating plague. Muwatallish thought that the plague had been sent by the gods for the wrong which he committed against Ramses and his subjects.[35]

But why was it that the Hittites apparently felt more guilty over aggression against a neighbor than did other ancient peoples? The answer seems to lie in their greater sense of security. The Hittites were well protected by the mountains in their homeland of Asia Minor. There too,

---

35. C. W. Ceram, *The Secret of the Hittites*, New York, 1956, p. 343.

they had ample deposits of iron ore and soon learned how to fashion iron weapons. With such formidable armaments, not only could they repel attacks, if necessary, but make inroads into foreign lands and build up a vast empire.

It was tragic that the Hittites instructed the Assyrians in the use of iron. It was almost as unfortunate that the Babylonians of Nebuchadnezzar's time also learned how to utilize it. However, another people, likewise familiar with iron, and before whom the new Babylonian empire fell, namely the Iranians, were again more humane. We may recall that Cyrus the Great (558-528 B.C.), upon capturing Babylon, allowed the captive Jews to return to their home. Furthermore, the Iranian monarchs rivalled the pharaohs in their concern as to how just they had been during their reigns. The later king, Darius the Great (521-485 B.C.), had the following epitaph inscribed on his tomb:

"Right have I loved, and wrong I have not loved. My will was that no injustice should be done to any widow or orphan, and that injustice should be done to widows or orphans was not my will. I strictly punished the liar, [but] him who labored I well rewarded."[36]

Again the higher ethical sense of a people was due to circumstances. While they were not in as secure a position as the Hittites, the Iranians were in a safer location than the societies living along the Nile and the Tigris-Euphrates. Therefore, when the Iranians subjugated their neighbors, they did not exploit them as severely as did the earlier imperialists. They neither taxed as exorbitantly, demanded as much in the way of forced labor, nor uprooted entire populations like their predecessors had. In effect, the Phoenician, Syrian, and Babylonian cities could prosper under Iranian rule.[37]

---

36. Breasted, *The Dawn of Conscience*, p. 345.
37. M. Rostovtzeff, *Social and Economic History of the Hellenistic World*, Oxford, 1941, Vol. I, p. 83.

However, the Iranians shared one thing in common with the Assyrians, Babylonians, and Egyptians. None of these societies had feelings of guilt over having undertaken conquest. But with the imperialists along the Nile and the Tigris-Euphrates, it was the belief that conquest was necessary for survival which rendered them immune to such feelings; in the case of the Iranians it was also the comparative mildness of their imperialistic policies which eased their conscience.

The freedom from guilt feelings was reflected in the religions of these four expansive societies and in their attitudes toward life. Their outlook was generally this-worldly and optimistic. The Babylonians and Assyrians prayed to their gods for an ample harvest, a life of abundance, good health, and victory when at war. They expected that after going through the appropriate rituals and making the necessary sacrifices, the gods would answer their prayers. And these blessings would come in the present life and not in the hereafter. The religion and attitude of the Egyptians was very similar. To be sure, these Nile inhabitants expected to enter a next world after death. But they did not regard this future abode as a haven from worldly cares and sorrows. Rather, it was a mere extension of their earthly existence.

The religion taught to the Iranians by the prophet Zoroaster (c. 650 B.C.) was likewise this-worldly; the thought associated with it was also hopeful with respect to life on earth. True, being late-comers on the historical scene and exposed to several different cultures, the Iranians were more philosophic than were the dwellers on the Nile and Tigris-Euphrates. Yet, their philosophy was essentially a happy one. Zoroaster saw the universe as a gigantic arena in which the forces of good are arrayed against those of evil. Leading the struggle for the good life is the Wise Lord, Ahura Mazda, whose principal adversary is the Evil One, Angra Mainyu. Man, however, is not merely a passive observer in this struggle but an active participant, and through his participation the forces of good and light will triumph in the end. In Zoroastrianism there was little room for resignation or despair. Life was considered worth living, and one was believed entitled to enjoy the pleasures and good things of the world. In the absence of guilt feelings, there was no place for celibacy, asceticism, or other forms of self-punishment, because they were not regarded as being necessary.

We shall now observe how decidedly the Iranian world view and perspective contrasted with the Brahmanist and Buddhist, in the East, and with the Christian, in the West. For in Brahmanism, Buddhism, and Christianity a virtual pessimism toward worldly existence has been the keynote, a pessimism which came as an answer to the guilt feelings of their devotees. Such mass guilty consciences followed eras of expansion and empire building, when exploitation and wanton cruelty were often the occasion.

Let us go first to the East and visit the Aryan invaders of India. Among them we may trace the evolution of Brahmanism and Buddhism and the gradual change in attitude from optimism to pessimism. What brought this about? It was their conquest of India and subjugation and humiliation of the Dravidian peoples.

Prior to their invasion, and even for a time thereafter, the Aryans worshipped primarily to enjoy the good things of the world. They prayed to their gods for fine weather, an abundant harvest, success in hunting and fishing, or in lovemaking, and a wholesome family life; they also asked for victory in battle. They gave little thought to the hereafter, nor were they interested in escaping from life itself. They were a vigorous folk, and their outlook was one of optimism.

To be sure, the Aryans did believe in a life after death. This belief was related to their ancestor worship. To them, having rebirth was as natural a phenomenon as was the continued presence of the ancestral spirit. Nevertheless, they were not obsessed with the desire to escape life and rebirth. They were not so obsessed because, as yet, they did not feel the need for self punishment. Such a need was to come after they imposed the caste system.

It is true that even before invading India, the Aryans maintained minor class distinctions among themselves. Their collection of hymns, known as the Rig Veda (1500–1000 B.C.) mentions the five occupations of soldier, priest, farmer, trader, and craftsman, but lines of demarcation among them were not well drawn.[38] With imperialism and conquest, however, the victors underwent marked social changes. The Aryan soldiers became more powerful. Indeed, many military leaders attained the rank of prince or even king; as such, they governed vast territories, lived in splendid palaces and had armies of retainers. The priests, though of the second class, became increasingly influential. They no longer presided over simple village ceremonies; instead they resided in cities and addressed huge throngs of temple-goers. Moreover, the ceremonies became so intricate that in order to conduct them much learning was necessary; this lore was the monopoly of the priests. As time went on, they also became wealthy.

Due to these developments, the social gulf between the soldiers and priests, on the one hand, and the Aryan farmers and merchants, on the other, became much wider. Most of the tillers and traders continued to live in modest circumstances; so, likewise, did the Aryan artisans, many of whom earned just enough for bare subsistence.

Yet, even the poorer Aryans were better off than the conquered Dravidians. The latter were compelled to work for the Aryan kings simply because they were the vanquished, and not because they had any special skills.[39]

38. Santosh Kumar Das, *Economic History of Ancient India*, Calcutta, 1925, p. 27.
39. J. N. Samaddar, *Lectures on the Economic Condition of Ancient India*, University of Calcutta, 1922, p. 53.

Furthermore, they were rigidly excluded from Aryan society and not even allowed to participate in the religious rituals. The Dravidians were once-born, the Aryans contended; only they, the conquerers, were twice born and, therefore, pure in thought and habits! The Aryans, alone, could look forward to rebirth in a higher class, now caste, provided, of course, they were moral and virtuous during their present life.

The vast majority of Aryans—almost all of the farmers, traders and craftsmen, and most of the priests and soldiers —viewed with pleasure the prospect of being born again into a higher caste or more comfortable circumstances. But for those who wielded power or lived in luxury this was not the case. Such rich or powerful figures began to meditate on their own lives. In so doing, they became conscious of how fortunate they were, especially when compared to the people whom they had virtually forced into pauperism or slavery.

It was such self-reproach which led wealthy merchants and priests and, particularly, princes and kings to renounce the power, splendor, and luxury that they enjoyed at the expense of others. It was such self-criticism which induced them to relinquish their authority, leave their palaces and villas and forsake their pleasures. It was this irritation with oneself which caused them to live in the forests, eat and dress simply and be pious and humble. Herein lay the basis of asceticism, which became such a characteristic feature of Indian life. Concerning the tendency of the rich and powerful, in India, to become ascetics, Professor Fick has this to say:

"Not only did world-sick old people renounce the world but even kings who were in undisputed possession of sovereignty and in the fullness of their power; young princes preferred the severe life of the ascetic to the glitter of sovereign power; rich tradesmen gave away their riches and heads of families their wives and children in order to build a hut in the forests of the Himalaya and to live on roots and fruits or to eke out an existence by begging alms."[40]

By renouncing their way of life, the rich and powerful were atoning for their feelings of guilt. This was the psychological basis of the Samkhya philosophy, Jainism and Buddhism. In these philosophical and religious systems not only were affluence and luxury severely criticized but the curtailing or (in the case of Jainism) even the complete suppression of sensual desire proposed as the means of securing peace and tranquillity. The founders of these three systems—Kapila (c. 650 B.C.), a scholar of the soldier caste; Mahavira (c. 600 B.C.), a high-ranking member of that caste, and Prince Gautama Siddhartha (555-485? B.C.)—considered sensual desire as leading to frustration and sorrow. Each of these savants sought relief from the world of physical wants and pleasures, and each had a different answer as to how this could be obtained. Kapila and the later Samkhya thinkers found the solution in realizing that the true self (*purusha*) is forever distinct from matter (*prakit*). Mahavira and the Jains went further. They contended that the soul (*atman*) must be liberated from the body, and to achieve this, a life of extreme austerity is necessary. Gautama Siddhartha took an intermediate position. He stressed neither knowledge nor a rigid asceticism but recommended an eightfold path of virtue. In treading this path, one limits but does not completely suppress his sensual wishes.

While the Samkhya philosophy was too scholarly and the Jain religion too severely ascetic to attract many adherents, the more moderate and yet mystical Buddhism flourished. It was at least tolerated by the Emperor Chandragupta Maurya (c. 325-291 B.C.), the founder of the first great Aryan empire in India, and during whose reign

---

40. Richard Fick, *The Social Organization in Northeast India in Buddha's Time,* University of Calcutta, 1920, p. 67.

it drew many converts. A century later, it was openly
espoused by his grandson, Asoka (273-232? B.C.), who had
been an eyewitness to misery and suffering. Like his grand-
father, Asoka was a great empire builder. However, in the
course of one successful military campaign, such a huge
number of the enemy were wounded and slaughtered that
it weighed upon his conscience. He thereupon renounced
worldly values and became converted. In the following
inscription of the Emperor Asoka, we can see how the
desire to repent brought about his conversion to Buddhism:

"The country of the Kalingas was conquered by King
Prizadarsi (Asoka), Beloved of the Gods, eight years after
his coronation. In this war, in Kalinga, men and animals
numbering one hundred and fifty thousand were carried
away captive from that country, as many as one hundred
thousand were killed there in action, and many times that
number perished. After that, now that the country of the
Kalingas has been conquered, the Beloved of the Gods is
devoted to an intense practice of the duties relating to
Dharma (truth) among the people. This is due to the
repentance of the Beloved of the Gods on having conquered the country of the Kalingas."[41]

Two later conquerers and empire builders—Kanishka
(second century) and Harsha (seventh century)—were
also won over to the new faith, and for the same reasons.
Kanishka, a Scythian ruler, took advantage of the internal
strife in northern India to pillage and subjugate the country; Harsha, a native-born prince, restored order in Hindu-
stani in the short span of six years, but after ruthless
military exploits; both became devout Buddhists.

True, in India at least, Buddhism eventually declined
in popularity. By criticizing the caste system and the Brahman priest hierarchy it sealed its own doom. Still, it had
much in common not only with Jainism and the Samkhya

41. D. C. Sircar, *Inscriptions of Asoka*, Delhi, 1957, pp. 51–52.

philosophy but also with the idealistic Brahmanism which supplanted it. All of these schools renounced the good things of the world and, with them, worldly cares. All of them (except the Jain, which already preached a rigid austerity) became increasingly ascetic as feudalism emerged and the caste system hardened.

The rising asceticism in the official Brahmanist creed is well indicated in the ensuing passage from the Manu Smrti (Laws of Manu), which date from about the first century A.D. Here, a middle-aged man of the twice-born castes is told how he should live if he wishes to be even worthy of rebirth, let alone of unity with Brahman, the World Spirit:

"When a householder sees his skin wrinkled and his hair gray, and when he sees the son of his son, then he should resort to the forest.

"Having given up food produced in villages by cultivation, he should depart into the forest, either committing his wife to the care of his sons or departing together with her.

"Having consigned the sacred fires into himself in accordance with the prescribed rules, he should live without a fire, without a house, a silent sage subsisting on roots and fruit."[42]

Brahmanist idealism attained to a new height in the eighth century A.D. It was then that Sankara, a philosopher and religious teacher, introduced the Platonist Vedantra Sutra system. In this most mystical of the Brahmanist Six Systems, all sensory impressions are considered to be not only frustrating but illusory. To Sankara the only reality is Brahman, of which other substances and events are mere images. Significantly, Sankara lived at a time when feudalism was making great inroads and the caste system had indeed become rigid. Significantly, it was an age of monas-

---

42. *Records of Civilization: Sources and Studies,* ed. Wm. Theo de Bary, New York, 1958, LVI, p. 234.

ticism, asceticism, and celibacy flourished as never before.

Continuing our Eastern tour in ancient times, and crossing the Himalayas from India to China, we notice a decided difference in the religions and perspectives of the Indian and Chinese societies. Whereas the Indian upper castes became deeply pessimistic toward life, the Chinese ruling class remained generally optimistic. Why was this so? The answer can be found in the very nature of the Chinese social system after the country had been unified.

To be sure, China, like India, was invaded and occupied by powerful clans coming from the northwest. But the invaders were not as racially distinct from the aboriginal settlers in China as were the Aryans from the Dravidians. This meant that a caste system never developed to the extent that it did in India. It meant further that the Chinese upper class had less reason to be disturbed by feelings of guilt.

The era of expansion in China opened with the conquest of the country by the Hsia clans; this occurred at about 2750 B.C. The Hsia conquest was followed much later by the Shang (1760 B.C.) and finally by the Chou 1122 B.C.). From 1000 B.C., if not earlier, Chinese society was divided into two classes—a nobility and a peasantry. The nobles referred to themselves as Chun Tzu (sons of the lords) and to the peasants as Hsiao Jen (lesser men). The Chun Tzu lived in walled cities and administered the territories which the *wang* (king) entrusted to them; the Hsiao Jen were farmers who rented small plots of earth from the administration.[43]

Quite possibly, the nobles were descendants of the conquering clans, but there is little evidence to support this. Even if true, however, the vanquished were not humiliated to the extent that the Dravidians were. To be sure, the

---

43. C. P. Fitzgerald, *China: A Short Cultural History,* New York, 1950, p. 60.

Hsiao Jen were tenants rather than proprietors. But they at least were tillers of their rented farms and not laborers who were at the complete disposal of the wang or of his aristocratic governors.[44] Furthermore, the Chinese Hsiao Jen were not looked upon as outsiders and impure. The Aryans, in India, maintained that they alone possessed souls and were twice-born. In China the "lesser men" had, along with the "sons of the lords," a definite place in the scheme of things. From the advent of the Hsia the nobles worshiped *tien* (heaven) and regarded their king as the "Son of Heaven"; the common people revered the earth god, She. From this difference in the object of devotion a dualistic concept arose. The heaven principle, or *yang*, came to represent the aristocracy and masculinity; the earth principle, or *yin*, the peasantry and femininity. Still, though the nobles were higher in status, the peasants were considered to be just as vital to the economy and society.

Admittedly, in the later centuries of the Chou Dynasty (1122-255 B.C.) many of the peasants faced severe poverty, but their impoverishment was owing more to soil conditions than to social oppression. The exhaustion of the soil, due to the dry climate, the lack of vegetation, and wind and water erosion was a problem of which the court and the provincial administrators were only too well aware. This is evident in the energetic steps taken by them in the effort to relieve the situation. They drained or reclaimed additional land, encouraged the planting of new crops and forbid any soil to lie fallow.[45] While these measures met with only partial success, their enactment indicated that the ruling class was, at least, worried about the difficulties confronting the peasant.

Since it did not oppress the lower class as severely as

44. Mabel Ping hua Lee, *The Economic History of China,* Columbia University, 1921, pp. 44-45.
45. Lee, *The Economic History of China,* pp. 46-47.

did its Indian contemporary, the Chinese upper class felt less guilty; hence, its scholars were not nearly as idealistic, pessimistic and otherworldly. Chinese thought, in contrast to Indian, stressed ethics rather than metaphysics; it was concerned with life in the present world instead of in the hereafter; it sought social reorganization and not individual salvation. In fact, most of the hundred schools of philosophy which arose in the sixth century B.C. were proposals as to how to solve the grave problems—economic, political and moral—which were facing the realm.

And grave they really were! For by then, China had become the scene of almost chronic warfare. Province fought province, clan fought clan, and family fought family. At times the turmoil was so great that nobles were murdered in their very chambers by those whom they had regarded as trusted servants. Often the individuals so trusted, and in vain, were their own generals, so closely did the country border on chaos.

The first eminent philosopher to suggest a solution was Confucius (551-479 B.C.) . To him, the only way to bring order out of chaos was to restore the human relationships which existed from ancient times. Subjects should respect their rulers; wives, their husbands; children, their parents; younger brothers, their elder brothers; friends, each other. Furthermore, not only should the people do honor to their rulers and ancestors, but the sovereigns, in turn, should treat their subjects as children.

More progressive than Confucius was his principal pupil Meng K'o, or Mencius (372?-289? B.C.) , who saw the rulers and their governments as having been frequently to blame for China's woes. In fact, Mencius advocated the overthrow of a regime if it ruled unwisely, although in other respects he generally agreed to the opinions of his teacher.

Whether progressive or conservative, however, the significant fact is that Chinese philosophy was concerned primarily with both the material and moral improvement of society, and there was lacking the fervent call for asceticism that one found in India. In the following passage from the "Book of Mencius," we can readily see how different the Chinese view was from the Indian as to what constitutes an ideal life for the middle aged:

"Let the five mu of land surrounding the farmer's cottage be planted with mulberry trees and persons over fifty may all be clothed in silk. Let poultry, dogs and swine be kept and bred in season and those over seventy may all be provided with meat. When the aged wear silk and eat meat, and the common people are free from hunger and cold, never has the lord of such a people failed to become king."[46]

Even the few Chinese schools which tended toward mysticism were essentially optimistic and this-worldly. An excellent illustration of this were the Taoists. Tradition states that the founder of Taoism was Lao Tzu (b. 604? B.C.), but he is probably legendary. Rather, its principal teacher, at least, was Chuang Tzu, who lived in the fourth century B.C. To Chuang Tzu, the solution to China's difficulties lay in conceiving the Tao, or moral law, and this by meditating and living quietly but comfortably. However, the conception of the Tao was supposed to benefit society as well as the individual. For it meant that one should help his fellow men by being modest toward them and by not taking more than his just share.

A century following the appearance of Chuang Tzu's works speculation as to how order could be restored gave way to positive action. The disintegrating empire was forcefully reunited under the Duchy of Ch'in, the most powerful state in the country. Under the Ch'in dynasty, the feudal order was swept away and what remained of the nobility, after the chaos of the late Chou period, was

---

46. *Records of Civilization*, Sources and Studies, ed. Wm. Theo de Bary, LVI, p. 234.

virtually liquidated. The Ch'in emperor, Shih-huang-ti (246-210 B.C.) was succeeded by the Hans (206 B.C.-220 A.D.), who, during their first century of rule, were equally energetic. In fact, the Han emperors embarked upon imperialistic ventures in order to improve economic conditions at home. Imperialism, however, meant war, taxation, frequent impoverishment of the peasant, and occasional famine.

It was here that Buddhism was introduced into China. Having appeared first at the court of the Emperor Ming-ti (65 A.D.), it didn't become firmly rooted in the religious soil until the third century. This was the century which saw the collapse of the Han empire; it was a century when the gulf between landlord and peasant became very wide; it was an age when Buddhism, with its tendency toward asceticism, celibacy and monasticism, won a number of converts, particularly from the more fortunate members of society.

Still, the influence of the otherworldly Buddhism was more limited in China than were similar creeds in India. Among the wealthy, it had to share its popularity with Confucianism; among the poor, with a transformed Taoism. Then too, it was often blended with the Confucianist or Taoist creed. The Buddhist Dharma (truth) and Sangha (community) were interpreted to mean the Confucian Doctrines of Filial Piety (respect for one's ruler, elders and parents) and of the Mean (exercise of self-control in public affairs). Or the Buddha himself was raised to divine status and became identified with the several or more gods worshiped in the later form of Taoism, deities whose devotees were members of cults and secret societies. Thus, even the Chinese Buddhists were more interested in establishing an orderly state or in seeking a means of belonging in a mystery cult than they were in practicing asceticism. But then this trend was merely a reflection of the social system in China—the absence of caste, especially from the later centuries of the Chou dynasty and in the ages following. This situation is thus summarized by Dr. Latourette:

"In spite of the strength of the family tie and of all these many organizations (clans, business associations, etc.), Chinese society has been characterized by a remarkable minimum of hard and fast class divisions. The sharp distinctions between the aristocrat and commoner which seem to have existed at the dawn of China's history largely disappeared long ago, probably shattered in the prolonged disorders which brought the Chou dynasty to an end and further erased by the autocrats of the Chin and the Han. . . . The continued development under later dynasties of a system of choosing officials from those who had proven their worth in the free competition of the public examinations militated against the formation of an hereditary ruling caste."[47]

Concerning this trend in China, the following description by Dr. Lin Yutang is also interesting:

"The redeeming feature is the absence of caste and aristocracy in China. And this brings us to Fate. . . . We Chinese believe that every dog has his day and 'heaven's way always goes round'. If a man has ability, steadiness and ambition, he can always rise and climb high. Who can tell? A bean-curd seller's daughter may suddenly catch the eyes of a powerful official or colonel, or his son may, by a strange accident, become the doorkeeper of a city magistrate."[48]

Here lay the basis for the minimum of guilt feeling and of the need for self-punishment among the upper classes in China. Here, too, was the reason for the realism and common sense which have characterized Chinese thought.

---

47. K. S. Latourette, *The Chinese, Their History and Culture,* New York, 1947, p. 683.
48. Lin Yutang, *My Country and My People,* New York, 1935, p. 198.

So far in our Eastern tour we have contrasted the guilt-ridden and idealistic princes and priests of India with the less remorseful and more realistic aristocrats and magistrates of China. Suppose we were to compare either with the rulers and nobles of early Japan? We would then discover that the Japanese court and nobility could be placed in an intermediate position. For when the conquering clans from whom the rulers and nobles were descendant—the Yamato—established their hold on the country, they didn't subject the older inhabitants to severe humiliation; on the other hand, neither did they allow them to till the soil. In a word, they were neither as ruthless as the Aryans in India nor as relenting as the Hsia, Shang, and Chou in China. This was because the various warring tribes were not separated by color, as in India, but only by mountain barriers, a situation which was even less the occasion in China.

In the course of the conflict the victors seized the lands of the vanquished and compelled them to become the wards or clients of the Yamato chieftains.[49] While the Yamato considered themselves to be Ryomin (good people), they referred to their clients as Semmin (base people).[50]

Conquest and consolidation by the Yamato, however, did not necessarily mean peace. For Japan, in the sixth century A.D., was like China in the sixth century B.C., a scene of warring noble families. True, there was an emperor who claimed descent from the sun goddess Amaterasu ome Kami, the chief goddess in the Shinto pantheon. True, the emperor had an elaborate court and a body of officials who were entrusted with the task of enforcing the imperial decrees. Yet, the sovereign had more prestige than actual power. It was all that he and

---

49. Y. Takekoshi, *The Economic Aspects of the History of Civilization in Japan*, London, 1930, Vol. I, pp. 48–49.
50. G. Sansome, *Japan: A Short Cultural History*, London, 1936, p. 40.

his officials could do to keep the warring nobles and their respective clans from disrupting the empire. The flames of warfare, in which the arrows and swords did their deadly work, were fanned by the local pride and sentiment which persisted within the circle of each clan. Such sentiment was rendered acute by the lofty mountains and rugged coastline, so characteristic of the Japanese scene.

The emperor was truly anxious to bring about peace. So were his leading ministers, that is, theoretically. For actually the ministers derived much benefit from the continued strife. Most of them came from the very influential Soga clan, and still it was from the Soga that other clans friendly to them secured their generals. Hence, the Soga reaped the profits made through the blood shed by others. Frequently, their reward was a huge estate taken from a fallen rival. Meanwhile, at the other end of the social scale, the clients of all the nobles remained as poor as ever.

This whole state of affairs perhaps weighed upon the conscience of the Soga minister, Iname. It certainly disturbed the Crown Prince Shotoku (573-621), who at the time was heir to the throne. Though the prince had no part in the baneful drama which was being enacted both on the stage and behind the scenes, he nevertheless felt responsible.

It was here that the prince sought comfort in a new religion. Though, like all Japanese, he believed in the gods and goddesses of Shinto, he very likely felt that the creed itself was not sufficiently otherworldly and renunciatory to offer consolation or the means for retribution. During his leisure hours the prince was an avid student of foreign culture, and in the course of his studies he became interested in Buddhism. His interest developed rapidly after the court had received from the king of Paikche, in Korea, several scriptures and images of the Buddha, together with the following message regarding the new faith:

"This doctrine is amongst all doctrines the most excellent. But it is hard to explain and hard to comprehend. Even the Duke of Chou (earlier ruler of China) and Confucious had not attained to a knowledge of it. This doctrine can create religious merit and retribution without measure and without bounds, and so lead on to a full appreciation of the highest wisdom."[51]

Soon, Prince Shotoku invited Buddhist missionaries to his court and not much time elapsed before Buddhism was adopted as the official creed.

It was hoped for by many that with the establishment of Buddhism as the official religion the internal strife would, at least, be minimized. This wish was only partly fulfilled. For while there was less in the way of armed conflict, another problem arose. In the seventh century the Soga were overthrown by the emperor, with the assistance of the Fujiwara clan. During the next three hundred years, it was the Fujiwara who controlled the affairs of state. They not only monopolized virtually every political office but held a huge amount of property, which they had seized from their enemies. The Fujiwara and the clans related to them formed the bulk of the aristocracy, while far below them in rank were the lesser Yamato clans, whose members were ordinary farmers. Due to high taxes and to corruption in political circles, the farmers found it difficult to retain their small holdings.

The Fujiwara and the other nobles, aware of their privileged position in society, contributed generously to the building of Buddhist temples, monasteries, schools, hospitals, and orphanages. Concerning the tendency of the Japanese upper class to make such heavy endowments at this time, Professor Sansome states:

"The most striking feature of early Japanese Buddhism is the enthusiasm with which members of the ruling class devoted their energies and their wealth to building monas-

---

51. The *Nihongi*, trans. W. G. Aston, London, 1956, pp. xix, 34.

teries and chapels, to filling them with precious objects, and to indulging a strong taste for imposing ceremonies, performed by numerous monks in the richest of vestments. It was a common practice for the heads of great families to endow shrines for the benefit of their parents, living or dead, while less important people dedicated images or made votive offierings, with prayers, for the happiness of their relatives, in this life and the next."[52]

By dedicating shrines to their ancestors, parents and relatives, the nobles were, in a sense, atoning for them, as well as for themselves. This wish to atone could also be seen in the very nature of the Buddhistic worship. For at this time, a number of denominations arose, but all of them placed much stress upon learning and ceremony. Both the lore and the ritual were difficult to study; yet, as such, they fulfilled the psychological needs of the aristocrats, their very difficulty serving as a means of retribution. And retribution from them was forthcoming, in view of the great luxury with which they were surrounded.

Meanwhile, the political picture was again changing. This time the scene of the drama was on the northern frontier. Here, the Yamato clans, with the assistance of forces dispatched by the court, were carrying on a series of campaigns against the aboriginal Ainu. After a protracted struggle, these clans finally won a decisive victory over them and, as a result, acquired all of the territory south of present-day Sendai. This triumph strengthened considerably these northern clans. Eventually, one of the most powerful of these groupings—the Taira—seized control of the government, only to be ousted later by another and even more formidable military clan—the Minamoto.

The campaigns and power seizures by the military clans caused Japan to become feudal. In 1185 Yoritomo Minamoto, whom the emperor had appointed shogun (generalissimo) , established his government at Kamakura, far

52. G. Sansome, *A History of Japan to 1334,* London, 1958, p. 65.

from the court at Kyoto. Yoritomo entrusted his *bushi* (warriors) with the task of governing the different districts of the empire. Thus, the emperor lost what little authority he had exercised, and the aristocracy became politically impotent. At the other end of the social scale, many farmers were forced, through heavy taxes, to become the serfs of more powerful landowners; the latter were bushi of the Minamoto and related clans.

With the establishment of feudalism, new sects of Buddhism arose to meet the needs of the times. Several of these denominations met the necessities of the farmers and serfs, one, those of the warriors.

So far in our discussion, I have spoken of Buddhism and of most otherworldly faiths as appealing principally to the upper classes. However, in my treatment of Chinese history, I did indicate that if adhered to in a certain way, these faiths could offer the lower classes consolation. This they could do by merging with the more popular cults and, thereby, permitting their followers to become intimate with one or several gods. Some of the Chinese Buddhistic sects did just that by referring to the Taoistic deities as manifestations of the Buddha. This was likewise the occasion in Japan. Two of the Japanese Buddhistic sects—the Tendai and the Shingon—identified the Buddha with the goddesses and gods of Shinto. But in order that the temple goers could feel such a sense of belonging to one or several gods, a simplified ceremony and course of study were needed, a worship that did not require so much in the way of elaborate ritual and intensive comprehension.

Such a simplification in both ritual and lore was introduced in the twelfth century, with the appearance of the Shinshu, Jodo, and Nichiren sects. All three were migratory and resembled in one way or another the early Aryan creeds of India, the later Taoistic cults in China, and the Greek mysteries. The Shinshu maintained that there is only one form in which the Buddha appears; at the same time, it considered faith alone as being sufficient for communication with him. On the contrary, the Jodo and Nichiren sects believed that the Buddha could appear in several different forms, but required that their members repeat a simple phrase to secure contact with him, the Nichiren even going so far as to include a loud chanting and beating of drums in its ceremonies. All three denominations drew large followings from among the serfs and farmers of feudal Japan.

As for the warriors, there was a special sect which found favor with them. This was the Zen, also introduced at this time. In contrast to the other denominations, the Zen emphasized severe mental and bodily discipline. Only after undergoing such rigorous training, they believed, could one find the Buddha within him. What did this training consist of? It involved certain distinct practices— sitting for hours in a definite position, going without food or sleep, and concentrating on a single object. These practices were applied in addition to the customary Buddhistic abstention from eating meat and working on animal materials.

Why was there such a severe regimen, and why did it appeal especially to the bushi? At first, it would appear that its purpose was not only self denial but self-punishment. However, its aim was more practical. The warriors felt that only through such training could they justify their newly exalted position in society. The bushi believed that since the gods had appointed them to high political office, they had to prove their mettle. This meant avoiding the luxury and corruption which had brought about the downfall of the nobles. For by practicing austerity they could show those under their jurisdiction that they were capable of governing them; in this way they could justify their exalted status in society. Thus, Dr. Nitobe writes in his account of Bushido (the way of the warrior) :

"A feudal prince, although unmindful of owing reciprocal obligations to his vassals, felt a sense of responsibility to his ancestors and to Heaven. He was a father to his subjects, whom Heaven entrusted to his care."[53]

It was the chief of the bushi, in effect, the shogun himself, who allegedly had been given the greatest responsibility, and he had to prove himself worthy of his trust. Thus, the later shogun, Ieyasu (1600-1616) stated in a conversation with one of his governors:

"The Shogun must not forget the possibility of war in peacetime and must maintain his discipline. He should be able to maintain order in the country; he should bear in mind the security of the sovereign (emperor) ; and he must strive to dispel the anxieties of the people."[54]

To shoulder these burdens the shogun had to discipline himself and limit severely his desires and pleasures.

Accordingly, the discipline of the bushi, or samurai, had both a worldly and religious basis. Although there persisted the tendency to renounce life, the purpose of the discipline was also to train men to live like ideal warriors and administrators. In a word, Bushido and Zen Buddhism were self-depriving; however, the self-deprivation was not only an act of retribution but the means by which the warrior class sought sanction from the gods for its lofty position.

Concluding our travels to the ancient East, we saw how the ruthless imperialism of the Indo-Aryans weighed on the conscience of their upper castes and caused many of the princes and priests to become pessimistic toward and even renunciatory of life. We further noted how the more moderate policies of those who conquered and unified China induced their scholars and officials to remain optimistic and practical. We finally observed that the nobles of Japan became, to an extent, otherworldly and contributed

---

53. I. Nitobe, *Bushido, the Soul of Japan,* Tokyo, 1908, p. 35.
54. *Records of Civilization: Sources and Studies,* LIV, pp. 338–39.

generously to the Buddhistic movement, and that the later warriors disciplined themselves severely, both as an act of retribution and to justify their administration; doubtless among them there was optimism and pessimism.

Touring the ancient West, we would notice a similar contrast. We would see how the Greek perspective in Alexander's day, and for a century following, contrasted with the Roman (and Greek) in the time of Constantine. Whereas the Greeks of the Hellenistic age were optimists and realists, the Italians and Greeks of the late Roman empire became Christians and, as such, looked upon the world as an abode of sin and evil. Why was there this discrepancy? Because the motives for and the nature of Hellentistic imperialism differed considerably from those of the Roman.

There were several motives for Alexander's conquests. One was his wish for adventure and esteem. Another was his desire to spread Greek culture throughout the Orient. But an equally, if not more important, consideration was the overpopulation of Greece. The Greek soil was too poor to support the thriving city-states, and these communities were compelled to import foodstuffs. To do so the cities had to sell their own products, but competition and war rendered sale difficult. Thus, Alexander and the Graeco-Macedonians were urged on to world domination largely by economic necessity.

Alexander did not live to consolidate his conquest of the Persian empire; after his death the Macedonian generals divided up the seized territories. But the imperialistic policies of these successors—the Ptolemies and the Seleucids—were comparatively mild. For they generally left conditions in their new domains as they had found them.

In Egypt almost all of the land had been divided between the pharaoh and the temples; the rest was held by feudal lords. The Ptolemies simply took the place of the pharaohs and permitted the peasants to rent land from the royal house or from other landlords, as had been done before.[55] True, the Hellenistic rulers did demand, each year, from all of the peasants so many days of forced labor, but the pharaohs had made use of the corvee from early times. Only toward the temples were the Ptolemies more severe than had been their predecessors. They assumed far greater control of the temple administrations, in order to regulate their industries and secure revenue. However, these religious organizations were extremely wealthy and, under the later pharaohs, had been unduly grasping.

In Syria (which included Palestine and Babylonia) the Seleucids were also careful not to change the land tenure systems. Throughout the Syrian domain, there were temple lands, noblemen's estates, and also many villages of free peasant proprietors. To be sure, the rulers did occasionally, but not frequently, confiscate temple lands and grant them to court favorites or high officials. Furthermore, they did the same with the estates of the nobles, though again not so often. But the free peasant proprietors were unmolested.[56]

The moderate policies of the Hellenistic monarchs indicated that the Greek colonists came to the Orient to earn a livelihood but not to rob the natives. In fact, the wealthier of the Greek colonists and the native priests and nobles together constituted an upper class. Their families mingled freely, and there was frequent intermarriage. They all met and assembled in such lively commercial centers as Alexandria, Damascus, and Rhodes.

These three centers were also places of great learning, where science, art, literature, and philosophy flourished. Not only did they flourish, but their very spirit was optimistic, realistic, and this-worldly, though the opposing

---

55. Rostovtzeff, *Social and Economic History of the Hellenistic World*, p. 278.
56. *Ibid.*, p. 512.

trend was there to a minor degree. I have already referred to philosophic realism as existing in the Hellenistic world; needless to say, the art and literature showed the same tendency. In the field of literature, the prose novel took the place of the poem, the characters portrayed in the novel were from all walks of life and not just from the aristocracy, while the plots had less of the fantasies which were found in stories elsewhere. In the realm of art, human and animal figures were painted or carved in a manner true to nature; even their facial expressions were decidedly realistic. In neither the art nor the literature was there evident an urgent desire to escape from reality, an attempt which was so noticeable in societies where idealism, pessimism, and otherworldiness had become interwoven into the cultural pattern.

The prevalence of realism in the Hellenistic world was due, of course, to the growth of intercontinental trade, the opportunity for many individuals of different cultures to exchange opinions and the remarkable achievements in science. For within the several Hellenistic empires and smaller kingdoms there were a number of interactive societies—the Greek and Phoenician city-states and the Lydians in Asia Minor. Interaction, as we have seen, was conducive to realism and this-worldliness. However, such a common sense attitude could prevail only in an atmosphere where the conquerers were rather free from guilt feelings and the consequent urge to escape into a hereafter or renounce all existence.

The Macedonian and Greek conquerers of the Middle East were quite different from the Roman imperialists who succeeded them. For the Romans, unlike the Hellenists, created an empire largely for the purpose of material gain rather than economic necessity. What proof do we have of this? First of all, Italy, even prior to the Roman conquest of the near Orient, was a flourishing region. The southern half of the Italian peninsula was,

along with Sardinia and Sicily, the richest source of grain
in the Mediterranean world.[57] Here, there was also much
in the way of commerce and craftsmanship. Since this
entire area was under Roman domination, Rome was already a wealthy city-state. Secondly, in the course of their
empire-building, the Romans pillaged and destroyed such
rival commercial centers as Carthage, Syracuse, and
Rhodes, the last-named city never having really been hostile to Rome. Thirdly, the policies pursued by the Romans
after they acquired their vast domain indicated their
prime motive for conquest. In hardly any other imperialistic state of ancient times was there as much cruelty for
the sake of sheer profit; in none was the enslavement of
peoples carried out on such a vast scale.

When the Roman legions took possession of Greece,
Asia Minor, greater Syria, and Egypt, they were ordered
by their commanders to carry off hordes of farm animals,
a huge number of implements, and, from the cities, countless treasures. They were also told to take thousands of
prisoners, to be sold later into slavery.[58] Even the subsequent consolidation of Roman rule did not put an end
to the greed of the commanders. Being nobles of the
senatorial order, the most honored group in society, they
were appointed governors and administrators of the provinces. In this capacity, they exacted enormous levies
through a tax farming system, which created severe hardship. But the senatorial class was not the only one to
become enriched from the plunder. Just below it in status
was the equestrian order (order of the wealthy), consisting
of merchants and landowners who had become prominent
since the second war with Carthage (218-201 B.C.) and
who were now able to reap substantial fortunes by lending
money at high interest and serving as provincial judges

57. M. Rostovtzeff, *Social and Economic History of the Roman Empire,*
    Oxford, 1926, p. 9.
58. Paul Louis, *Ancient Rome at Work,* London, 1927, pp. 122-23.

and magistrates. Such mass plunder marked the last two centuries of the republic.

The succeeding rule of the emperors (31 B.C.-476 A.D.) was, in the long run, just as disastrous. True, the plundering had ceased, except when the provinces revolted. But the taxes were just as exorbitant. Then too, much of the land became the property of the imperial household, military commanders and nobles alike. On their estates the new owners hired those who had lost their holdings; often, the persons so engaged were reduced to serfdom. Such was Roman policy in the eastern half of the empire.

In the western half it was equally oppressive. Throughout North Africa, Spain, Gaul, and Britain, Roman nobles and capitalists acquired huge farms and plantations, and former legionnaires received holdings of moderate size. On these establishments the owners employed slaves who had either been prisoners of war or had been natives that were captured in frontier raids. Because of competition with slave labor, and often of coercion, the village economies in these western provinces were ruined. Indeed, the native villagers, having been rendered destitute, were themselves often forced into serfdom. While in Africa, after the destruction of the tribal economy, the number of independent native landowners was drastically reduced, in much of Spain and in Gaul and Britain they all but disappeared.[59]

Roman imperialistic policy was soon felt in Italy. There, what was a sturdy yeomanry had to abandon its holdings because of competition with the huge grain farms in the provinces. Its place was taken by nobles and wealthy commoners, who dotted the Italian countryside with extensive ranches, olive groves and vineyards. Meanwhile, in desperation, the landless farmers migrated to Rome. In the capital they became an idle proletariat, which was fed on free grain and sadistic amusements. Such sadistic

59. Rostovtzeff, *Roman Empire*, p. 297.

pleasure was to be had by seeing the triumphant return
of a Roman army, with its glittering treasures taken as
booty and long lines of prisoners burdened with chains,
or by watching the gladiatorial combats with their fights
to the death. Psychologically, such spectacles were highly
compensating to the proletariat.

The question now arises as to why the Romans, and
particularly the Roman upper classes were so strongly
motivated by the desire for profits. In answering, we may
say that the cause lay in the rivalry between the nobles
and the wealthy commoners, a rivalry which arose after
Rome had defeated Carthage. Although the nobles of the
Roman republic, being descendants of patricians and rich
plebians, controlled the senate, and this means the government, the non-aristocratic merchants and landowners were
also becoming powerful and influential. Hence, the aristocracy, fearful that the plutocracy would overtake it, was
spurred on to new conquests, both in the east and in the
west. By recoming wealthy in these ventures and living in
splendor, the nobles of the senatorial order could retain
their status in society and continue to draw a line of demarcation between themselves and the rich commoners of
the rapidly rising equestrian order.

Yet, as we noted, the latter were not slow either in
obtaining huge profits from Roman expansion. Moreover,
not far below the plutocrats there was an urban middle
class, which likewise was attempting to scale the economic
and political ladder. The members of this class, too, were
seeking to reap a rich harvest by exploiting the people in
the provinces. In this way they also could aspire to high
political office, at least in their own communities, live in
sumptuous villas and be prominent in society.

Due to the mass exploitation of the provincial population, many Romans and even a large number of non-
Roman Italians of the upper and middle classes were soon
able to enjoy luxuries and live in a manner which their

ancestors would have considered immoral. Gone was the simplicity and frugality of earlier times and the strict observance of taboos. Instead of eating and drinking in moderation and offering food to the gods in earnest, they ate and drank to excess, with the food offering becoming a mere formality; instead of maintaining purity of habits, they committed adultery, even near a sacred fire; instead of having kept within the civic boundaries, they erected a veritable world empire. In effect, the Romans, having become completely an expansive society, openly violated the conventions handed down to them from the migratory age.

The Romans, however, were not without their stern critics. Against both their plunder and the change in their manner of living were voices, literary voices, raised. Virgil (70-19 B.C.), the leading poet, denounced those among his fellow citizens who pillaged for gold and whose only concern was for riches, luxury, and fame:

"One wreaks ruin on a city and its hapless home, that he may drink from a jewelled cup and sleep on Tyrian purple; another hoards up wealth and broods over buried gold; one is dazed and astounded by the Rostra; another, open-mouthed, is carried away by the plaudits of princes and of people rolling again and again along the benches. Gleefully, they steep themselves in their brother's blood; for exile they change their sweet homes and hearths and seek a country that lies beneath an alien sun."[60]

Horace (65-8 B.C.), another eminent poet, likewise took the Romans to task, but his criticism was directed at another aspect of life in his day—the decay of manners and morals:

> With pliant limbs the tender maid
> Now joys to learn the shameless trade
> Of wanton dancing and improves

---

60. *Georgics*, from Virgil, *Works*, trans. H. Rushton Fairclough (Loeb), 1956, II, pp. 500–14.

> The pleasures of licentious loves;
> Then soon amid the bridal feast
> Boldly she courts her husband's guest;
> Her love no nice distinction knows,
> But round the wandering pleasure throws
> Careless to hide the bold delight
> In darkness, and the shades of night.[61]

In a more somber tone, Horace also referred to the crimes committed by the Romans and to their facing possible punishment by the gods for these misdeeds:

> Though guiltless of your father's crimes,
> Roman, 'tis thine, to latest times
> The vengeance of the gods to bear,
> Till you their awful domes repair,
> Profaned with smoke their statues raise,
> And bid the sacred altars blaze.[62]

Soon the protests against the cruel and vulgar phases of Roman life became louder. They were no longer confined to the literary circle, but spread to and profoundly influenced philosophic and religious thought. And these protests appeared among all classes.

Especially did the state religion feel their impact. For in Rome, and among the Roman colonists in the provinces, there was a growing indifference to the state creed, and particularly to emperor worship. True, there was still a show of reverence toward the Graeco-Roman gods and goddesses, and elaborate temples were erected to Jupiter, Mars, Apollo, and Minerva. Yet the worship itself was coming to be more in the nature of a formality and was losing its appeal among an ever larger element of the populace. Many Romans, other Italians and even a large number of Greeks were becoming aware that the creed which was centered in the traditional pantheon was not meeting the needs of the troubled times.

---

61. Horace, "To the Romans," in *Odes,* trans. Philip Francis, London, 1831, Ode VI.
62. *Ibid.*

Many of those in high society, disgusted with the gluttony, depravity and greed displayed in their midst, but unable to find consolation in the contemporary religion, retired to the realm of mind and meditation. In so doing, they usually became either Stoics or Platonists. Both schools drew a large following, particularly from among the upper classes and intellectuals. Among the Stoics there was the naturalist, Pliny the Younger (62?-114?) ; the nobleman and playwright Seneca (4 B.C.-65 A.D.) ; the highly educated slave and essayist, Epictetus (50-138 A.D.) ; and the Emperor Marcus Aurelius (161-180 A.D.) ; among the Platonists there were the philosophers, Philo Judaeus (25 B.C.-50 A.D.) and the later Plotinus (205-270 A.D.) . As Stoics and Platonists they held that one's soul is more vital than his body, and to the rich this meant a repudiation of everything which they enjoyed, often to the detriment of others. Such a stern disapproval of pleasure was forcefully expressed by Epictetus:

"When you get an external impression of some pleasure, guard yourself, as with impressions in general, against being carried away by it; nay let the matter wait upon your leisure and give yourself a little delay. Next, think of the two periods of time, first, that in which you will enjoy your pleasure, and second, that in which after the enjoyment is over, you will later repent and revile your own self; and set over against these two periods of time how much joy and self satisfaction you will get if you refrain."[63]

While a number of cultured persons in the upper class were turning to philosophic idealism, a fair proportion of the lower, freemen as well as slaves, were seeking another means of belonging. This they were doing by joining migratory, or mystery, cults. What were these different cults and where did they come from?

There was the cult of the sun god Mithra, introduced from Iran; there were the rituals in honor of Magna Mater

63. Epictetus, *The Discourses, as Reported by Arrian,* trans. by W. A. Oldfather, (Loeb) , 1946, No. 34.

(the Great Mother), having originated in Asia Minor; there were the ceremonies to Isis, the Egyptian goddess of fertility; to mention only the most popular. These cults were similar to the Greek mysteries, which were also drawing a large following. Like the Orphic and Eleusinian mysteries the Oriental were also attempts to seek communion with a supernatural being and thereby gain immortality. At the Oriental ceremonies, too, the devotees took bread and wine, which represented the body and blood of the adored deity. To be a member of a cult one likewise had to remain chaste for a certain length of time and undergo periods of fasting. Only in this way could they be rid of impurity and sin. Membership in a cult was open to all, and class distinctions were nonexistent.[64]

Christianity, too, was purely a mystery cult at first. This it became almost immediately after the crucifixion of Jesus, regarded by many Jews as having been their Messiah. It was because they so regarded the Nazarene that Paul and the other Apostles came to believe that he had risen from the dead and obtained immortality. This belief they transmitted to their disciples. Not long afterward, the disciples maintained that if one wished to become immortal, he should participate in the Eucharist—the chanting of hymns and the partaking of bread and wine (the body and blood of Christ). When assuring its devotees of immortality, the Christian creed did not promise a Nirvana, in the Buddhist sense, but rather a veritable paradise. And a paradise was what numerous underprivileged people in the Roman empire were hoping for.

Christianity, with its increasingly large following from among the poor and illiterate, came under sharp attack from the learned elements of the population. It was scored by those who were adept in Greek philosophy and who, in particular, were followers of Plato. Hence, to meet this attack, it adopted certain features of Platonism. Like the

64. J. B. Carter, *The Religious Life of Ancient Rome,* Boston, 1911, p. 83.

latter, Christianity came to distinguish between the Idea and the visible world, this distinction is applied to its own doctrines. To the Christian leaders the Platonist Idea became identified with the God of the Jews, and the Logos, or transmitter of divine reason, with Christ. Soon it was but one more step to acknowledge Jesus as the Son of God. Thus, within a century following the advent of Paul (64 A.D.?), Christianity had become both other-worldly and idealistic, the one characteristic offering the poor a means of escape from a hostile world, the other providing the more literate, at least, a philosophic basis for the new creed.

Still, in order for the new religion to be successful, most of the wealthy Romans and more fortunate among the Italians and Greeks had to be won over. Aside from the poorer farmers, proletarians, slaves, and some of the literati, the senatorial aristocrats, capitalists and workshop masters also had to be converted. And it was in the late second and third centuries that the conversion of the prominent and wealthy occurred. It was then that not only merchants and shopowners, but rich landowners, and even those of noble birth, turned to Christianity. This trend was observed by Origen (185-254), who, at the time, was one of the leading Christian theologians in Alexandria.[65]

Why did so many nobles and rich commoners become converted in the second and third centuries? Because there was introduced into Christianity a new doctrine, a doctrine that allowed the more fortunate citizens of the empire to atone for their feelings of guilt. These individuals, living in such comfortable circumstances, were only too well aware that they had been violating the morals handed down by their ancestors, who had lived simply and frugally. They had also become aware that it was wrong to

---

65. Origen, "Origen Contra Celsum," in *Writings of Origen*, trans. Rev. F. Crombie, Edinburgh, 1910, Vol. II, Bk. III, Chap. IX, p. 92.

kill or enslave others, not in self-defense, but for the sake of profit. What the workshop masters, merchants and aristocrats needed was a doctrine which would condemn not only pleasure but man himself and thereby urge him to make retribution. This is how Christianity came to adopt the idea of Original Sin.

In a sense, the doctrine of Original Sin dated back to the Hebrews. For in the Old Testament, Adam and Eve were punished for having stolen the forbidden fruit from the Garden of Eden. The belief that God would punish anyone who had sinned against Him was very strong among the Hebrews, although similar ideas were harbored by other migratory peoples. However, the punitive measures were limited to Adam and Eve and not applied to their descendants. The Jews believed that only when their entire nation had committed a sin, would it, as a whole, be liable to suffer penalty.

With the spread of Christianity, Adam's disobedience to God's command came to have a deeper meaning. In the New Testament, which was written early in the second century, mankind was regarded as having rightfully deserved the misery with which it was confronted. Man, justifiably, was living in a chaotic world. Such chaos was of his own doing, because, from the time of Adam, he had chosen to depart from God's way.

However, it was in the late second and early third centuries that man himself was looked upon as being tainted with sin. Just as a child receives his body from those of his parents, so also from their souls does he inherit his. As Adam was the first man, so did his descendants inherit from him their guilt-ridden souls. With this idea, set forth by Tertullian (c. 155- c. 222 A.D.) and Cyprian (c. 200-c. 258), two prominent Christian clergymen in Carthage, and later by St. Augustine (353-430 A.D.), humanity as a whole was considered as being inherently evil and worthy of condemnation.

The making of such an assertion fulfilled a very basic

psychological need for those who possessed great wealth and held high rank, in the late Roman empire. For in asserting that man is by nature a sinner, one admitted that he had done wrong, an admission by which he punished himself and, in part, overcame his guilt feelings. I say in part, because the admission itself was insufficient as a means of atoning completely. To further redeem himself he had to do penance. This meant observing the seven sacraments and thereby showing faith in the Son of God, in the Savior, who had atoned for the sins of mankind. In this regard, Tertullian and Cyprian also maintained that Christ, through his sacrifice, had saved man from eternal damnation.

Thus, the background of the empire's conversion to Christianity reveals, at first, a ruthless conquest, followed by severe feelings of remorse and the dire need to atone. This sequence was well summarized by the poet, Prudentius (348-c. 410). Commenting on the final conversion of the empire to Christianity, Prudentius contended that Rome, in so doing, was repenting for both her past imperialism and her persecution of the early Christians:

"For the first time in her old age, did Rome become teachable and blush for her long history, ashamed of her past and hating the years gone by with their foul superstitions. Then, when she recalled how the lands that bordered on the ditches under her walls had been wet with the innocent blood of the righteous, and saw around her thousands of accusing tombs, she repented still more of her harsh judgment, her unbridled acts of power, her too great anger in the cause of a base religion. She sought to make up for the shocking wounds of injured righteousness by showing a late obedience and asking for pardon. Lest her great power be under the charge of cruelty because she rejected goodness, she sought the prescribed atonements and with entire love passed over to faith in Christ."[66]

---

66. "A Reply to Address of Symmachus," from Prudentius, *Works*, trans. H. J. Thomson (Loeb), 1949, I, 510.

While imperialism and the need to repent formed the background of Christianity, the growth of feudalism caused it to flourish. For the confusion and chaos wrought by an emerging feudal order impelled more and more inhabitants of the Empire to seek consolation through the Church.

It was particularly in the western half of the Empire that feudalism was emerging. Why? Because, first of all, the western provinces had less access to foreign markets than did the eastern and could not be assured of a steady flow of wealth. Secondly, the west had had to import slaves to offset the shortage of labor, and, as we noted, it was the use of slaves by wealthy planters and shopowners which caused the small proprietors to disappear. With the demise of the middle class, purchasing power rapidly declined and interprovincial trade all but ceased. Wealth became scarce, and due to lack of funds, the scope of imperial administration was narrowed to the more prosperous eastern half; in the west, each locale became independent, politically as well as economically. With the establishment of the feudal system, in the fifth and sixth centuries, we leave the ancient world and enter the medieval.

To summarize, we noted in our account of Christianity how it served the needs of those who had been ruthless in their imperialism and felt the urge to repent. In this respect, the Christianity of the western Aryans compared with the Buddhism and Brahmanism of the eastern. However, there was one very vital difference between the western and eastern faiths. Whereas Buddhism and Brahmanism sought only the renunciation of earthly existence, Christianity condemned the very nature of man. Why was there this difference? Because the people who profited from Roman imperialism had inevitably a much deeper sense of guilt than did those who benefited from the Indo-Aryan. Among the Romans, other Italians, and Greeks, far more than among the Indo-Aryans, were there wealthy landowners, investors and shop masters who had committed crimes against foreign societies, and for the sake of enrichment rather than for mere survival. Also, those who had committed such crimes had had a deeply influential migratory past, so that their very depravity weighed heavily upon their conscience. This too was less the occasion among the Indo-Aryans, whose migratory age had not been as restricting. One indication of this was that the Indo-Aryans appeared to have had more sexual freedom than did the early Greeks and Romans.[67]

But then the Aryan princes and warriors who subjugated India had, in turn, greater cause to feel guilty than did the rulers and aristocracies of expansive societies other than the Roman. This was owing to their imposition of a caste system and to the ample time which they had to reflect on their actions. This is why they, too, became increasingly negative in their consideration of earthly existence.

The guilt feelings of the Aryan upper caste compared with those of the Yamato rulers and nobles of Japan. For the Yamato had imposed a near caste system and were frequently at war. Hence, they too were converted to an otherworldly faith.

By contrast, the kings and aristocrats in Egypt, Asia Minor, Iran, and China had less desire to underscore either their earthly existence or man himself. The reason was that they were somewhat more considerate of their subject peoples. They were not obsessed with a desire for profit, nor were they faced with a "color problem" and the wish to impose a caste system. The Babylonian and Assyrian rulers and their retainers also did not feel the urge to repent. But in their case it was certainly not because of moderation in imperialistic policies; rather it was due to the apparent necessity of policing surrounding areas. Thus, it was inevitable that the religions of these societies would, for one reason or another, differ from Buddhism, Brahmanism, and Christianity.

To be sure, there were in Brahmanism, Mahayana

---

67. R. Briffault, *The Mothers*, London, 1927, Vol. I. p. 346.

Buddhism and Christianity aspects which appealed to those in humble station: the sense of affinity with a divine being and the promise of a happy hereafter. But these migratory features found favor with those who had suffered rather than profited.

4

Crime and Self-Punishment In Medieval Europe

In the preceding section, I spoke first of the ancient *migratory* societies, then of the *interactive,* and finally of the *expansive.* In so doing, I indicated that there was an evolution in thought and conscience from the one group of societies to the next. The migratory were devoid of any sympathy for foreigners, while the interactive were only slightly sympathetic. It was only some of the expansive which felt compassionate toward foreign tribes and states, and then after they had subdued them. This was due to a relaxation of tension after having attained mastery. However, in the process of subjugating the imperialists became fully aware of the misery they inflicted. Consequently, they welcomed religious creeds which gave them the opportunity to atone.

Passing from the ancient world to medieval Europe, we may note that the sequence of events was almost the same. The earliest societies were migratory, suspicious and hostile. Several of the later states were expansive, and while continuing to be tribal in feeling and sentiment, at least had a sufficient conscience to be converted to Christianity. Often the kings of the expansive states were among the first to be converted. In accepting Christianity they were influenced by their wives, who, being more sensitive than their husbands, were particularly anxious to atone for the ruthlessness of their warriors. Countless nobles and knights also felt the need to ease their conscience. For having plundered enemy villages and put their inhabitants to the sword, they were deeply troubled. So great was their desire to atone that they joined monasteries, but this was a later development.

For the present, let us consider the early migratory peoples of Europe.

A. The Celts and Teutons of their Migratory Ages

In my account of the Roman empire I spoke principally of the peoples living along the Mediterranean and gave special attention to the Italians and Greeks. For as far as the Celtic settlers of Gaul and Britain were concerned, I mentioned them only in connection with their early attack on Rome and with later Roman expansion. But what was the mode of life among the Celts, or Gauls, in Caesar's day, and also among the Teutons, who lived beyond the boundaries of the Roman empire? What, in particular, were their customs and taboos, and how did their observance contribute to the future practice of Christian asceticism?

The Celts, in common with all migratory peoples, were fearful of both nature and of alien tribes. Hence, they depended very much upon the good will of their gods, especially in time of extreme peril. For example, those who contacted severe illness or were about to go into battle sacrificed animals or even men to the gods to receive their blessings.[1] These sacrificial rites were performed by their priests, or druids, who were held in high esteem. The druids compared with the Roman augurs, except that they were credited with having even more magic power. The

---

1. Julius Caesar, *Commentaries on the Gallic and Civil Wars*, Bk. VI, Ch. XVI.

druids, it was believed, could not only determine which days were best for conducting business or engaging in warfare but look into the future. Among the Celts, in Ireland, so lofty was the status of these priests that a king would not address the court until his druid had spoken first.[2] The advice of the court priest was sought continually, both in time of peace and in the event of war.

Toward enemies, or even strangers, the Celts showed little consideration. Indeed, the robbing and pillaging of neighboring tribes and settlements were encouraged to maintain discipline.[3] But this attitude would not have existed had it not been for a deeply rooted in-group feeling fostered by fear and anxiety.

The anxiety of the Celtic tribes could be attributed to the difficulties of living in the northern plains and forests, to mutual distrust and, in the case of the Gauls, to pressure from the Teutons, or Germans, farther east. However, the Teutons themselves were also apprehensive. With them it was the problems of living in forests and swamps, of intertribal warfare and of pressure from the Slavs and Huns. Of course, their customs and taboos likewise reflected this apprehension.

While the Germans didn't place much value on sacrifices, they went to extremes in practicing augury. Especially curious was their custom of looking for omens and auspices in the behavior of white horses. These animals were kept in woodlands and groves, where they were harnessed to sacred wagons. There they were watched by the tribal chiefs or priests, who observed their neighings and snortings and thereby interpreted the will of the gods.[4]

It was thought that if a man wanted to make a really favorable impression on the gods, he had to perform deeds of military valor. If a woman wished to please the god-

---

2. T. G. E. Powell. *The Celts*, London, 1958, p. 157.
3. Caesar, *Commentaries*, Ch. XXIII.
4. Tacitus, *Germany and its Tribes*, 10.

desses, she had to remain chaste until marriage; indeed the men of the tribe generally avoided a woman who had not done so.[5] If a family wished to be considered virtuous, it had to be hospitable toward fellow tribesmen. The display of valor and hospitality and the observance of chastity —these were regarded as the cardinal virtues. All three of these norms had their bases in the struggle for survival. Warfare was looked upon as a normal state of affairs; battles could be won only if the women didn't lure the men into sexual acts, and, significantly, both the men and the women married late in order to retain their youthful vigor.[6] Finally, refusal to share one's food with a kinsman was considered, in the light of an ever threatening shortage, a criminal act.

Raiding the villages of other tribes and carrying off food and livestock, however, were allegedly not criminal acts. In fact, such marauding expeditions were often undertaken to spy on enemy territory.[7] Like the Celts, the Teutons were not too disturbed over having committed such acts of aggression, so potent was tribal affinity and so prevalent were mutual distrust and hostility.

Later, several of the Celtic and Teutonic tribes entered the expansive stage, and in the next section I shall relate the steps which led to their conversion to Christianity. Meanwhile, however, we may assume that their migratory customs and taboos found their way into subsequent Christian practice. The Teutonic stress upon chastity found expression in celibacy, and Germanic hospitality led to self privation with respect to food; both were salient features of Christian asceticism. Also, the tendency of the Celts to submit to their druid priests could be discerned in the inclination of most Christians to conform to Church teachings.

---

5. *Ibid.*, 19.
6. Tacitus, *Germany*, p. 20.
7. F. Owen, *The Germanic People*, New York, 1960, p. 121.

B. The Teutons in Their Expansive Era

In discussing the migratory peoples of early western Europe, we had to consider both the Celts and the Teutons. But in relating the expansive, we may limit our scope to the latter. For although the Gaelic Celts, after migrating to Ireland, gradually subdued the native Picts and other early comers, they could hardly be regarded as empire-builders. With some of the Teutonic tribes, however, it was a different story. Among them the most formidable, with respect to size, quality of weapons, and organization, succeeded in subjugating many of the peoples around them.

Of all the Teutonic tribes or kingdoms, there were three that were able to undertake expansion in the grand manner. They were the Franks, the Saxons, and the Norsemen. Each had their beginning years of conquest, when they were either converted to Christianity, or, if having already been brought into the fold, in some other way repented. Each had a subsequent era of imperialism, during which time they underwent feudalization and experienced a marked growth in their Church organizations, trends which were not unrelated.

The Frankish conquests were first undertaken by Clovis (481-511), the chief of the Sicambri tribe, and who, through ruthless and cunning methods, was able to become king of the Salian Franks. Thereafter, he embarked on a policy of imperialism. He led his armies first against the Romans and then in battle with other Germans.

In all of his conquests, Clovis resorted to barbarism and cruelty. His lack of mercy is illustrated during the war with Syagrius, the independent Roman governor of the territory lying between the Loire and the Somme. Having defeated Syagrius in battle, and learning that his enemy had fled to the camp of Alaric II, king of the Visigoths, Clovis demanded that the refugee be turned over to him.

Alaric complied, whereupon Clovis had Syagrius promptly put to death.[8] With his seizure of the remaining Roman lands in Gaul, Clovis secured possession of the Seine valley and the town of Paris.

Clovis next turned his attention to the Alemanni tribes, who occupied both banks of the Rhine. After two great battles he and his army all but annihilated them and thereby made further additions to the realm. Moreover, with this eastward thrust, Clovis began a movement which saw other German tribes incorporated in to the Frankish state.

It was during his conflict with the Alemanni that the king of the Franks accepted Christianity. Whether all during this time he was disturbed by his greater cruelty and barbarism we do not know. We do know, however, that long before the outbreak of the war, his wife, Chlotilda, an orthodox Christian, had tried repeatedly to convert him.[9] Furthermore, we may assume that in preaching Christianity to him, Chlotilda and the Gallic clergy had spoken of sin and salvation. Thus, the historian Gregory of Tours indicates that in receiving baptism, Clovis was attempting to cast out evil. He describes this momentous event:

"And now the King first demanded to be baptized by the bishop. Like a new Constantine he moved forward to the water, to blot out the former leprosy, to wash away in this new stream the foul stains borne from old days. As he entered to be baptized, the saint of God spoke these words with eloquent lips: 'Meekly bow thy head, proud Sicamber; adore that which thou hast burned, burn that which thou has adored.' "[10]

With the conversion of the Franks, the most powerful of the German kingdoms was brought into the fold. Since the

8. L. Sergeant, *The Franks*, London, 1898, p. 105.
9. *Ibid.*, p. 143.
10. *History of the Franks*, trans. O. M. Dalton, Oxford, 1927, II, p. 69. Quoted from James W. Thompson and Edgar N. Johnson, *An Introduction to Medieval Europe*, 300–1500, New York, 1937, p. 109.

Frankish realm soon extended to the Pyrenees as well as to the Rhine, the effect of this conversion was profound.

While the Franks were building an empire on the continent, three other Teutonic peoples, less important but equally stubborn, were consolidating their conquests in Britain. Who were these invaders? They were the Jutes, from Jutland in Denmark; the Angles, from present-day Schleswig; and the Saxons, from the region of the lower Elbe. The Jutes were subsequently confined to the district of Kent; so we may practically dismiss them. The Northern and Middle Angles were more formidable, and in the seventh century had succeeded in carving out the larger kingdoms of Northumbria and Mercia, respectively. But the Angles had a powerful rival in the West Saxons, whose kingdom of Wessex was destined to attain supremacy. Hence, it is the West Saxons who concern us most.

The beginnings of West Saxon expansion date from the reign of Caedwalla (686-688), and of his more gifted successor, Ine (688-726). Caedwalla was as cruel as he was ambitious, and yet, during his brief kingship, he repented. The historian Bede gives this interesting account of how he and his army subjugated the Isle of Wight and then made amends for it:

"After Caedwalla had possessed himself of the kingdom of the Gewissae (West Saxons), he also took the Isle of Wight, which till then was given over to idolatry, and by cruel slaughter endeavored to destroy all the inhabitants thereof, and to place in their stead people from his own province; having bound himself by a vow, though he was not yet, as is reported, degenerated in Christ, to give the fourth part of the land, and of the booty, to our Lord, if he took the island, which he performed by giving the same for our Lord to the use of Bishop Wilfrid, who happened at the time to have accidentally come thither out of his nation."[11]

---

11. *Ecclesiastical History of the English Nation*, trans. J. Stevens, rev. J. A. Giles (Everyman) 1958, Bk. IV, Ch. XVI.

It is interesting that after having struggled so hard to win the crown, Caedwalla abdicated at the end of two years. It is highly significant that upon his abdication, he journeyed to Rome to be baptized.[12]

Ine, on his part, conquered the neighboring kingdom of Kent and even pushed beyond the borders of Celtic Cornwall. Yet, when he was not in the thick of battle, Ine was busy framing legal codes, and his laws were the earliest in West Saxon history. However, this useful act alone seemed to him insufficient for salvation, and following an eventful reign, he, too, made a pilgrimage to Rome.[13]

In the ninth century the West Saxons established their jurisdiction over England, but only to lose it eventually to the Danes. The last renowned King of Wessex, Alfred the Great (871-901), a mighty warrior as well as able law-giver, more than held his own against them. But almost within a century, Knut the Great (1016-1035) had added England to his Danish dominion.

Knut, in all probability, was a near descendant of Rollo (c. 911-c. 931) who with his kinsmen plundered the northern counties of Frankish Gaul. Finally, through a treaty concluded with the Frankish king, Rollo gained possession of Normandy, and, in effect, became the first Norman duke. One of the provisions of the treaty was that Rollo and his chieftains accept Christianity; hence they took the holy vows and became baptized. Perhaps they did so as a matter of expediency, or just as likely, they wished to atone, in some way, for the crimes they had committed. However, from this time, the Norsemen, in northern France, were brought into the fold.

Thus far I have spoken of the exploits of Clovis, the Frank; the Saxons, Caedwalla, Ine, and Alfred; and the Norsemen, Knut and Rollo. Still, they were only in the vanguard of the expansive movement. Rather, it was their

---

12. *Ibid.* Bk. V, Ch. VII.
13. *Ibid.*

successors who carried these imperialistic policies to a successful conclusion. It was they who extended the boundaries of their kingdoms until they were veritable empires. But this does not imply that these later kings were true monarchs. For they had repeatedly to contend with the rising class of feudal lords.

It was in the Frankish realm that feudalism first reared its head in the pool of society. This was when the successors of Clovis rewarded their nobles with sizeable fiefs for having rendered military service. The policy of granting fiefs was continued until eventually the seigneurs were powerful enough to oust the last of Clovis's descendants and turn the reins of government over to the mayor of the palace. The mayor, at this time, was Pepin the Short (751-768).

Pepin's most illustrious descendant was Charles the Great (768-814) who, early in his reign, rendered valuable assistance to the pope. Not only did he rescue the papacy from the Lombards, but he compelled the Saxons to become Christians. For his services, Charles was crowned emperor of the Romans by the pontiff, in 800. What a proud moment it was for him to have become a successor to the Caesars, and for his Franks to be the veritable descendants of Roman legionnaires! How elating it was to be virtually the standard-bearer of the Roman eagle!

But the western empire of Charles also went the way of the ancient Roman. It, too, underwent decline and dismemberment; in fact, its disintegration was even faster. For after the death of Charles, when his grandsons struggled for the crown, the feudal lords became the holders of immense fiefs; these the seigneurs apportioned among their vassals. At the close of the ninth century, the Frankish section of the empire was the scene of feudal strife and near anarchy.

A century following the advent of Charles, the idea of a Roman empire was revived by a distant German relative of the English West Saxons. This was Otto the Great (936–973), who, likes Charles, had saved the pope from his enemies and in 962 was crowned emperor of the Romans, as had the Frankish ruler.

True, the Holy Roman Empire, founded by Otto, lasted much longer than had the western of Charles. Indeed, it reached its apogee in the twelfth century, when it covered an area embracing most of present-day Germany, the Low Countries, Switzerland, Austria, Bohemia, and almost all of Italy. Its very magnitude was highly impressive.

Yet, the Holy Roman Empire was likewise bound to collapse under the impact of feudalism. The emperors were face to face with a losing battle against the dukes and counts of the empire, who, in turn, were supported by the popes and clergy. For the pontiff was interested in strengthening his own hold upon the country. By the end of the twelfth century, Germany, too, was a vast array of feudatories, both lay and ecclesiastical.

In contrast to the Franks and the Saxons, the Norsemen, or rather the Normans, were more successful in holding their empire intact. It was William the Conqueror (1066–1087) who established an empire, the Anglo-Norman, which better stood the test of time. Why? Because William, by a single stroke, had acquired in England a huge domain where he could be sole ruler by right of conquest. Yet, the Norman conquerer also introduced a kind of centralized feudalism, in which his seigneurs were given conditional land grants. Accordingly, the Norman seigneurs, too, reaped the fruits of imperialism.

What was the result of expansion as far as the rural masses were concerned? In a word, what was meat for the noble was poison for the peasant. The very occasions of conquest and confusion provided the aristocrats with the opportunity to rob the peasants of their holdings. Thus, the turmoil which came after the reign of Clovis saw the enserfment of many small Frankish proprietors; so did the closing decades of the western empire. It was the same story in the Holy Roman Empire, where before there had been a free Saxon peasantry. Finally, in England, following the Norman conquest, those who were modest farmers became serfs on seigneural estates.

How did this ever widening gulf between the lords and the peasants affect the Church? It made the Church even richer and more powerful than before. The peasants, having been reduced to near slavery and miserably poor, looked longingly for a passage to heaven and gave the local priests the little they could afford. But this wasn't all. In one way or another, the bishops and abbots coerced the poorer farmers into relinquishing their land. Hence, it was not long before the Church had a huge amount of property and thousands of serfs on its estates. Still, the pope and his prelates considered the accumulation of so much wealth to be fully justified in view of the Church's high spiritual office.

But while the Church officials could justify their intake of wealth from the poor, the lay nobles could not. To be sure, the priests themselves preached from their pulpits that God had so ordained for society to be divided into three classes—the clergy, the nobility and those who were under obligation to toil for the two upper orders. But at the same time, the seigneurs were constantly reminded that they could not give spiritual guidance to the serfs who lived on their manors. True, with their fortified castles and men-at-arms, they could give the peasants better protection from bandits, renegade soldiers or robber barons than could the Church authorities. But due to recurrent warfare among themselves, the seigneurs demanded much from their serfs in the way of crops and services. Of course, the peasants who suffered most were those whose fields and villages were ravaged by their lords' enemies.

Aware of their cruelty to each other and often to the peasants, and being without a spiritual role in society, the seigneurs sought to ease their guilt feelings by making retribution. How? One form of retribution I have already mentioned—the donation of gifts to the Church. Another and a very common form was the rendering of service to others. To be sure, the feudal system itself was founded upon pledges of loyalty and service such as those which a vassal made to his lord. The vassal, usually a lesser noble or knight, received a land grant from his lord, invariably a greater noble or king, in return for a sacred promise to provide men and arms when needed. But aside from these feudalistic obligations, there arose the practice of assisting the weak and helpless—orphans, widows and women, generally. Such consideration for the weak was expressed in the code of chivalry.

While the donation of gifts and practice of chivalry were the most usual ways of atoning, there was another that was far more extreme. This was the act of leaving the ranks of the nobility, altogether, and of joining or establishing monasteries. The earliest monastery was that of the Benedictines, founded at Monte Cassino, in the sixth century, but from the ninth there were many others throughout western Europe. The nobles who founded and became members of these orders could practice celibacy and asceticism and live in the manner of Christ and the Apostles. Consequently, it is not surprising that the monastic orders consisted principally of former knights and seigneurs.

In the following passage, the medieval historian Odoricus Vitalis tells how a count who served under Charles the Great atoned for his past deeds:

"In the year of our Lord, therefore 806, in the fifth year of the reign of the Emperor Charles, on the feast of Saints Peter and Paul, Count William became a monk and was suddenly changed and made another person in Christ Jesus. For after his profession, he was taught without being offended and corrected without being angry. He suffered blows and injuries unresistingly and without having recourse to threats. He rejoiced to be subject and delighted on every kind of humiliation."[14]

The period which saw the end of the western empire was one during which many hermit communities were founded, and by individual seigneurs. In 1080 the son of a viscount established just such a community at Muret, near Limoges. But more famous was the settlement of the Carthusians, founded by Bruno of Cologne (1030-1101), a man of aristocratic lineage. The Carthusian monastery was built on a lofty peak overlooking the town of Grenoble. Within the monastery each monk lived in his own bare cell, cultivated a small garden, ate very simple meals and spent much of his time in prayer and meditation. Only at prayer meetings and on Sundays did the monks meet together, as each one sought salvation for himself.[15]

Equally mystical and ascetic were the Cistercians, founded in Burgundy, and whose dominating personality was a renowned Burgundian nobleman, St. Bernard (1090-1153). The Cistercians also lived very cloistered lives, except that their meetings together were more frequent. Moreover, they likewise had many members from the upper classes. "Multitudes of noble champions and learned men joined their society from the novelty of its institutions and voluntarily submitting to their canonical rigor, rejoicing to chant triumphant anthems to Christ in the right way."[16]

France and Burgundy, however, were not alone in having nobles and knights who felt the need for repentance. For in the Germany of the twelfth century, the scene of

---

14. Vitalis, *The Ecclesiastical History of England and Normandy*, trans. T. Forrester, London, 1854, Vol. II, Bk. VI, Ch. III.
15. J. W. Thompson and E. N. Johnson, *An Introduction to Medieval Europe 300–1500*, New York, 1937, p. 610.
16. Vitalis, *The Ecclesiastical History*, Vol. III, Bk. VIII, Ch. XXVI.

an ascending feudalism and of frequent warfare, the monk and chronicler Caesarius von Heisterbach related the following episodes:

"The knight, Ludwig, who owned that castle which still frowns down on Altenahr, took the vows on his death bed and began forthwith to mend, contrary to the nature of his schemes, without sweating, or bleeding or sneezing, he just lived long enough to take the vows at Heisterbach."[17]

"Walther von Birbech was born in the town of that name, a man of great wealth and power and nobility, cousin to Henry, Duke of Louvain. He, in the heyday of his youth, being devoted to the knighthood of this world, wherein he was most doughty and renowned, was accustomed from his earliest boyhood, to call upon our Lady, the Holy Mother of God, and Ever Virgin Mary, whom he loved from the bottom of his heart, honouring her with fastings, alms givings and masses. At length, hearing that our Order was dedicated to the Blessed Virgin, he left, for her sake, all things in the world—riches, honours and friends—and took the cowl in the monastery of Hemmenrode, whose fame was then (as now) most renowned."[18]

Aside from France, Burgundy and Germany, Anglo-Saxon England also had her nobles who, at first, were even brutal and later humble. Again, the historian Vitalis related an interesting episode; this time the event having taken place in Mercia in the late seventh century:

"After a gentle childhood, when he (Guthlace) felt the impulses of youth and studied the valiant deeds of heroes, he collected his dependents and gave himself up to the career of arms, ravaging and destroying the villages and castles of his adversaries with fire and sword. Gathering immense booty, he made voluntary restitution of a third part of the plunder, for the love of God, to those from

---

whom it was taken. After pursuing this course of life for nine years, causing great losses to his enemies in person and goods, he began to reflect on the uncertainty of this mortal life and the instability of all human things, and coming to himself in a state of alarm and examining his conduct as if death was before his eyes . . . he renounced all worldly vanities and entered the monastery of Ripandun (in Cheshire), where he assumed the tonsure and clerical dress under the abess whose name was Elfrida."[19]

Not only the nobles but powerful kings, and especially those who had cruelly subjugated their enemies, had great misgivings. Thus, William the Conqueror confessed upon the approach of death:

"I tremble, my friends, when I reflect on the grievous sins which burden by conscience, and now about to be summoned before the awful tribunal of God, I know not what I ought to do. I was bred to arms from my childhood and am stained with the rivers of blood I have shed. It is out of my power to enumerate all the injuries which I have caused during the sixty four years of my troublesome life, for which I am now called to render account without delay to the most righteous Jesus."[20]

Doubtless, a number of William's viscounts and barons felt as he did. Therefore, even while still in the prime of life, many of them entered monasteries to ease their conscience. During the reigns of the Conqueror's successors, the monastic orders attracted countless individuals, and in the twelfth century they really flourished.

True, throughout western Europe, the monasteries became quite wealthy. Like the Church itself, the orders received much income through the sale of crops and of other commodities from their estates. No doubt, because their officials were from the privileged minority in society, rather than from the exploited majority, they had had

---

19. Vitalis, *The Ecclesiastical History*, Vol. II, Bk. IV, Ch. XVI.
20. Vitalis, *The Ecclesiastical History*, Vol. II, Bk. VII, Ch. XIV.

experience in managing estates. Yet, the fact that many in the upper class became monks and priests as a means of doing penance cannot be overlooked. Concerning the background of the clergy, Taylor states:

"Episcopal lands and offices were not inherited; yet, with rare exceptions, the bishops came from the noble fighting hunting class. . . . The same was true of the abbots. . . . As with the episcopal or monastic heads, so with the canons and monks. They too, for the most part, were well born."[21]

It was inevitable that a number of these former knights and nobles would retain their enthusiasm for war. And in answer to their need to engage in combat and yet atone by becoming monks, there arose the military orders. These organizations—the Order of St. John, the Knights of the Temple, and the Order of Teutonic Knights, to mention the most prominent—were brotherhoods, just like the usual monastic establishments. Only instead of living in solitude, their members went on military campaigns. In fact, they were often quite ruthless in their treatment of those whom they subdued. When the Knights of the Temple fought in the Holy Land, they were merciless toward their prisoners; when the Teutonic Knights conquered the region of the Baltic, they slew or enserfed the native people.

Such cruelty, so common in the Middle Ages, was due to the tendency to identify another with oneself and then mistreat him. One may say that it was self-punishment by proxy. The inclination to punish another in place of oneself explains the many sadistic acts—the trial by ordeal, torturing of prisoners, and public burning of heretics—committed during the medieval period. In effect, the urge to atone led to sadism as well as masochism.

This urge had its foundation in the expansion and in the war upon and exploitation of others, for which the

---

21. H. O. Taylor, *The Medieval Mind*, London, 1914, Vol. I, p. 489.

expansion was responsible. The warfare, and particularly
the exploitation, were contrary to the earliest of Christian
teachings, to those which were expounded when Christianity was still a migratory cult. Thus, the very nature
of the atonement which followed was such as to impose
restrictions that went far beyond those sanctioned by a
migratory people.

5

The Late Medieval and
Modern World:
Self-Denial Versus
Self-Gratification

So far, we have seen the effect on medieval Europe, of first, migration, and then expansion. Migration caused the Celtic and Teutonic tribesmen to band ever closer together; expansion, on the other hand, led to rigid class distinctions which cut across tribal lines and indicated vast differences in living standard. Migration induced the Celts and Teutons to maintain their traditional forms of worship; expansion brought about a conversion to Christianity and, on many occasions, monasticism, with its ascetic practices.

From the twelfth century, a new process was underway; at least it was novel to the medieval Europeans. This was interaction. With the interactive processes coming into play, and with the towns and town citizens appearing on the scene, the expansive social order—the Church and feudal state hierarchy—was in for trouble. The townsmen objected to a Church whose pope and clergy refused to recognize them as a class distinct from that of the peasants. They also were opposed to a state whose king and nobility were too privileged. The forthcoming assault on the pope and clergy led to the German and Scandinavian Reformations and the English Puritan Revolution; the attack on the king and nobility culminated in the French Revolution.

Protestantism, however, had different psychological antecedents than did Jacobinism. Since the Protestant movement was a defiance of the traditionally respected Church, it required justification in the form of self-denial. For the early Christians had practiced self-denial to atone for the crimes of ancient Roman imperialism, and the later reformers felt that they had to do likewise to justify their revolt. Jacobinism, on the contrary, was inspired by Humanism and the ensuing Enlightenment, rather than by Apostolic Christianity, and, also, its attacks were directed against members of the laity; accordingly, it needed far less justification. Hence, the Jacobins were more liberal in their attitude toward pleasure and put little stress upon self-privation. Hence, the people in Jacobin France and Humanistic Italy were more tolerant of self-gratification than were those in either Protestant Germany and Britain or rigidly Catholic Spain and Portugal.

In countries were the Europeans established colonies, there was rigid Catholic, Protestant, or Jacobin influence. At times, however, there were two influences, the one conflicting with the other. This was the situation in the later United States, where self-gratification was evidenced in a certain freedom of expression, but where, in the economy and in morals, self-denial had the upper hand.

Far beyond western Europe and America, there were political changes which induced a need for justification. This was the case in Japan, where the shogun and his warriors wrested control of the government from the court nobles, who traditionally were closest to the much revered emperor. To justify this action the earlier shoguns and their men-at-arms practiced austerity and maintained self-discipline. In early modern Japan, the same tendency to

justify governmental change by practicing self-denial persisted. But because of the milder nature of Buddhism, the
self-denial did not go as far as in Protestant Europe.

Accordingly, alongside my classification of societies into
migratory, expansive, and interactive, I have introduced
in this section another division: into those which were self-
denying and those which were more lenient toward self-
gratification. In this section, I will attempt to show that
the more rigid a society's social structure and way of life,
the greater its tendency to go to war and make conquests.
I will show that the expansive societies were more militant
than the interactive, the self-denying, generally, more so
than the self-gratifying. For restriction and regimentation
are contrary to normal human inclination, and, being
frustrating, easily induce aggression.

Aggression, however, can be directed toward either the
societies beyond or the power structure at home. On the
first occasion, war is the result; on the second, revolution.
The latter was more the case when the society itself was
divided into an expansive hierarchy and an interactive
mass basis, as in France under the Ancien Regime. It was
surely the situation when the societal unit was split between an expansive ruling order and migratory communities, as in Russia or China before each experienced a
communistic upheaval. For, unlike the Spaniards and Germans, the Russian and Chinese masses were not sufficiently
self-denying to support their expansive hierarchies. And
when, following their revolutions and the establishment
of neo-migratory societies, their anonymous members did
discipline themselves, it was not as an act of atonement,
but to benefit the group. Such discipline, nevertheless, was
also frustrating, to a degree.

The modern world has been the scene of war and conquest, and, as we shall note, the structure and way of life
of certain societies contributed much to this spectacle.

A. Interactive Forces in Medieval Europe and their Assault on the Church: The Practice of Self-Denial

The geographical circumstances of Europe are such as to encourage interaction on a wide scale. The small size of the continent, the exposure to numerous seas, bays, and channels, the countless inlets that can serve as harbor sites, and the many navigable rivers offer every inducement to trade and intersocietal contact. But the natural factors alone were not sufficient to promote interaction. For only after the Europeans had had a breathing spell from the recurrent warfare and invasion could commerce and communication become possible. Europe had such a breathing spell from the twelfth century.

Interaction, having thus begun, increased in tempo during the Crusades. For in their ventures to the Near East, the European nobles and knights became fascinated with the embroidered cottons, silks and satins, and cedar, ivory, and jewels which were being sold in the bazaars. Indeed, they were dazzled by the braided garments of fine texture and the sparkling gems that were on display. The news of these luxury items they brought back to Europe, where they informed other seigneurs and their retainers about them. Gradually, the demand for Asian as well as European products increased to such an extent that, in place of traveling merchants, there arose numerous communities of settled traders.

It was along the main avenues of commerce—the Mediterranean Sea and North Sea, and the Arno, Scheldt and Meuse rivers—that what were once mere villages on seigneurial estates developed into thriving towns. These urban communities appeared first in northern Italy, southern France and Flanders, and later, in southern England, eastern France and western Germany.

The rise of the town had far-reaching repercussions.

By their very nature and circumstances the towns were bound to be antagonistic to the feudal system, and this meant to the Church officials and lay lords alike. The towns stood for capitalism as against manorialism, a civilian and commercial order as against one which was military and agricultural. It was a conflict between commoners with movable wealth and aristocrats with landed property.

The bourgeoisie were not alone in their hostility to the feudal order. The kings, ever anxious to bring law and order to their realms, were also antagonistic to it. Because both the royalty and the bourgeoisie were so hostile to the feudal system they became allies in their attempts to curb the power and pretensions of the seigneurs. In England the Angevin and Lancastrian kings learned to depend on the townsmen for support; so did the Capetian and Valois kings in France and the monarchs in Spain and Portugal. In these alliances not only did the bourgeoisie lend money to the kings, but they even enlisted in or, at least, furnished recruits for the royal armies. Furthermore, in those countries, such as Germany, where the central government was no longer effective, the towns formed leagues for mutual protection. Thus, the bourgeoisie were at war with the feudal lords and most likely desired to see them eliminated altogether.

Aside from being hostile to the lay lords, the townsmen also felt a strong aversion to the clergy. A basic reason for this feeling was that feudal society, and this included the Church, didn't really recognize the merchants and artisans as a separate class but rather as upstart peasants. In the eyes of both the bishops and the barons, the urban dwellers had merely abandoned their farming, an abandonment which was morally wrong, since God had ordained that there were to be only three classes—the clergy, the nobility, and the peasantry. In fact, even the kings regarded the bourgeoisie as upstarts, while having them as allies.

No doubt, a number of the bourgeoisie also desired to

see the elimination of at least the higher clergy. But in harboring such sentiments, during the Middle Ages, they could not help feeling guilty. So what did they do? They established a moral sanction for their hostility to the Church. In revolting against the clergymen, they had to be more priestlike than they; those who revolted had to prove that they alone were following in the footsteps of the Apostles. In this respect, they resembled the monks and friars who were associated with the Church.

However, there was one basic difference between the older and newer ascetics. Whereas the friars and monks only sought security and salvation, the urban reformers wanted to change drastically the Church organization. Whereas the former only mildly protested against the fact that the clergymen didn't live up to their high ideals, the latter sought their actual removal. In a word, the newer ascetics were far more militant, and it is they who laid the groundwork for the Reformation.

As the Urban Revolution appeared first in Italy and southern France, so did militant asceticism. This was in the twelfth century. It was then that two radical reformers —Arnold of Brescia and Peter of Bruys—were among the earliest to protest vehemently against the abuses in the Church; in so doing, they advocated revolutionary changes. Arnold renounced the pope as a "man of blood who maintained his authority by killing and burning."[1] Because, he stated, the pope's conduct was so vastly different from that of the Apostles and early disciples, he did not warrant obedience. Peter of Bruys was equally radical; indeed, he was a forerunner of modern Protestantism. For he went so far as to assert that faith and individual character would alone assure salvation and that there was little need for "good works" or attendance at the ceremonies. Since the traditional rituals were unnecessary, so was the Church

---

1. J. W. Thompson and E. N. Johnson, *An Introduction to Medieval Europe 300–1500,* New York, 1937, p. 623.

itself! Needless to say, both Arnold and Peter were condemned and burned at the stake.

Yet such drastic punishment only served to spread the
heresies. In Lombardy, in the late twelfth century, a group
of artisans formed a brotherhood known as the Humiliati
—the Poor and Humble. These pious craftsmen bitterly
denounced the Church for its wealth and splendor and
lived in the manner of the earliest Christians. They wore
special clothing, slept on hard beds, ate very simple food,
and fasted frequently.

Soon the Poor and Humble were not alone. Their protests were echoed by the Franciscans in Italy and the
Waldensians in France and Bohemia. Both St. Francis
(1181-1226), who started the one brotherhood, and Peter
Waldo (d. 1197), who founded the other, were sons of
rich merchants, and their followers were from all walks
of urban life. The Franciscans were married to "My Lady
Poverty." They assailed the Church and the wealthier
monasteries for owning property. They possessed neither
churches, houses, nor land, and worked or begged for a
living. The Franciscans resembled the Waldensians, who
were called the "Poor Men of Lyons." The Waldensians
"never have settled homes, but walk two by two; they
travel about with bare feet, clothed in wool, possessing
nothing as individuals but holding all things in common."[2] At first, the Waldensians were mild in their protests
against the Church, but with their persecution they became far more erratic. Presently, they began to teach that
any layman, if sufficiently versed in the Bible, could preach
the gospel and conduct religious services. Eventually, the
Waldensians broke entirely with the Church.

While the Waldensian heresy was slowly spreading, the
more radical chapters of the Franciscans were winning
converts, notably in England. Here, more than a century
later, their most renowned preacher was John Wyclif

2. *Ibid.*, pp. 627–28.

(1324-1384). This eminent English reformer also attacked the Church ownership of property and administration of the sacraments. The popes Wyclif called "limbs of Lucifer"; the clergy he referred to as "fiends of Hell"; even the friars of the monasteries were regarded by him as "gluttonous idolators."[3] Wyclif, too, asserted that personal piety was sufficient for achieving salvation. His followers, known as Lollards, like other lay orders, denied themselves many comforts or even necessities.

From England Wyclif's ideas spread to the continent, and especially to Bohemia, where already the Waldensian heresy was rapidly making headway. Why Bohemia in particular? Because here the powerful bourgeoisie were very bitter toward the higher clergy. Not only did the latter refuse to recognize them as a class, but were German, and of the same nationality as the ruling Hapsburgs. Thus, the resentment was on both social and nationalistic grounds. So heated did this resentment become that it boiled over into the Hussite movement. John Hus (1370-1415), the man whose execution incited this famous uprising, was a veritable nationalist as well as religious reformer. And with the spirit of nationalism appearing on the historical scene, we are in modern times.

B. The Continued Assault on the Church: The Modern Reformation, English Revolution and Self-Denial

In the preceding chapter, we noted that the later religious reformers, mostly of urban middle-class origin, were more positive in their attitude toward life and a little less otherworldly than were the aristocratic monks and friars of the cloisters. Instead of withdrawing from the world about them the urban reformers attempted to change it. Such an effort was due to their feelings of hos-

---

3. *Ibid.,* p. 980.

tility toward feudal society, feelings attributable to their bourgeois background. For the bourgeoisie, the children of interaction, had little in common with the seigneurs, the offspring of expansion.

As the curtain opens on the modern scene, the forces of interaction are more active than ever. This means that the characters on the stage, though essentially the same as in late medieval times, played more positive roles than before. On the modern scene, there were numerous reformers, but they were still more concerned with the present life and with the affairs of the world than were their late medieval predecessors. To be sure, the modern, like the medieval, reformers, had certain qualms over having revolted against the Church. But the very manner in which they justified their rebellion differed considerably. Whereas the medieval Protestants practiced asceticism, or self-denial, for purely religious reasons, the modern did so in part for nonreligious and worldly causes. The modern reformers felt that in this way they could be more attuned to the times, while, at the same time, justify their revolt by making sacrifices.

What were these worldly causes? In a word, they were nationalism and capitalism. Nationalism entailed self-denial for the state, or for the sovereign of the state; capitalism meant privation in order to promote wealth. Both nationalism and capitalism were, therefore, self-denying. Yet, there was one vital difference between them. Since the nationalists glorified the state, they were completely loyal to the sovereign of their state, provided, of course, he was of the same nationality as his subjects. But with the capitalists, it was a different matter. Their concern was economic rather than political. They were interested solely in promoting business enterprise, and when a sovereign interfered with their efforts to foster economic growth, they sought his abdication, or a change of government if necessary. Thus, the seeds of religious revolt, which were nourished in the soil of interaction, eventually sprouted into either statism or political revolution.

Nationalism, or the finding of a common ethnic origin with others, is migratory in one sense, and interactive in another. It is interactive when compared to provincialism or tribalism, which is purely migratory. But then it is migratory when contrasted with the developing international and universal sentiment of the present age. Then too, we should bear in mind that without trade and communication, national feeling, let alone a thisworldly attitude, would never have arisen. And it is this feeling and attitude which distinguished the modern from the medieval Reformation.

Centering our attention on the modern Reformation, we soon become aware of the similarity between the Lutheran movement, in sixteenth-century Germany, and the Hussite in fifteenth-century Bohemia. Martin Luther, like John Hus, was opposed to the Church ceremonies; he, too, bitterly attacked the practice of selling indulgences. Luther also advocated the removal of the clergy and maintained that individual faith, and not "good works" and ritual, could save a man's soul.

But these religious convictions were not their only points of similarity. Both reformers were ardent nationalists and rebelled against foreign rule, whether secular or ecclesiastical. Hus appealed to his fellow Bohemians to throw off the Austrian Hapsburg yoke; Luther, in like manner, urged the Germans to rid themselves of the Latin clergy. Luther's nationalism was all too evident in the ensuing passages from his "Open Letter to the Christian Nobility." Here, he protested vigorously against the papal collection of the annates in Germany:

"Every prince, nobleman and city should boldly forbid their subjects to pay the annates to Rome and should abolish them entirely; for the Pope has broken the compact and made the annates a robbery to the injury and shame of the whole German nation."[4]

Finally, after denouncing the pope for other abuses, Luther concluded his letter by advocating a complete separation of the German Christians from the Roman Church:

"Since the Pope, with his Roman practices . . . usurps all the German foundations without authority and right and gives and sells them to foreigners at Rome who do nothing in German lands to earn them . . . the Christian nobility should set itself against the Pope as against a common enemy and destroyer of Christendom."[5]

Luther's call for independence, though addressed primarily to the princes and nobles, was answered by all classes in Germany. His pamphlets were read, by those who could read, in many a peer's manor hall, burgher community and peasant village. However, it was the nobles and, above all, the princes and Electors whom Luther, in turn, favored most in his sermons. For he and his pastors told their converts to be good subjects of their respective rulers, provided, of course, the latter were Protestants. "Obey your prince and do as directed," they said. Luther also told his followers to be content with their status in society, and such counsel was very pleasing to the aristocracy. Upon the burghers the Lutheran leaders did not look with as much favor, since they condemned certain business practices, such as moneylending. As for the peasants, Luther's attitude was all too clearly revealed during their revolt, in 1525, against the feudal lords. He was horrified at the very thought of social upheaval. "Smite, strangle or stab, secretly or publicly," he advised the nobles, and they did.

---

4. Luther, *Works*, trans. C. M. Jacobs, *et al.*, Vol. II, Bk. III, Sec. I, Philadelphia, 1916.
5. *Ibid.*, Bk. III, Sec. II.

Of all the German states it was in Brandenburg-Prussia that Lutheranism proved to be most popular among the ruling class. For in Prussia, especially, the practice of being dutiful to one's prince, humble before one's social superior and attending strictly to one's tasks was not new. Centuries earlier, the Teutonic Knights had imposed upon the inhabitants of Prussia an ironlike discipline, and this imposition left its mark. Now, with the Elector of Brandenburg and Duke of Prussia having accepted Luther's teaching, the later Prussian kings could command the greatest obedience from their subjects. It was in Prussia, too, more than anywhere else, that the peasant, and even the burgher, remained humble in the presence of the nobleman. Because of the power wielded by the Prussian ruling family—the Hollenzollern—a power which had religious sanction, and the prestige enjoyed by her Junkers (aristocrats), Prussia arose to a position of leadership throughout Germany.

The German princes were not alone in their espousal of Lutheranism. Due to similar circumstances, the kings of Denmark and Sweden also became imbued with it. The Danish and Swedish rulers, in the early sixteenth century, were trying to curb the power of their own nobles. Seizing Church property (as the German princes were doing) would enable them to overawe the barons and thereby bring about national unity in their respective kingdoms. Moreover, many of their subjects deplored the huge amount of wealth and property that had been amassed by the Roman Church. Consequently, first Denmark, under Christian III (r. 1523-1533), and then Sweden, under Gustavas Vasa (r. 1523-1560), were won over to the Lutheran cause. Shortly afterward, the kings in both countries gained the upper hand in their struggles with the nobles. Royal supremacy at home was followed by ascendance in international affairs. In the late sixteenth century, Denmark was the leading Power in northern

Europe; in the seventeenth, her place was taken by Sweden.

There was one vital difference, however, between the Scandinavian and German Reformations. In Scandinavia it was effected without the bitter religious struggle which was subsequently waged in Germany, a struggle which marked the Thirty Years War (1618-1648). As a result, Lutheranism in northern Europe did not remain as rigid in doctrine nor as puritanic in practice as it did in Prussia, Saxony and other German States. In the future, therefore, Denmark, Sweden and Norway became far more flexible in their social structures and tolerant toward religious minorities than did Germany.

While the Lutheran creed was becoming firmly implanted in the religious soil of north Germany and Scandinavia, the seeds of another Protestant faith—the Calvinist—were being sown elsewhere. Martin Luther and John Calvin had much in common. Both of them denounced the Church ceremonies and the issuance of the sacraments —in effect, the complete doctrine of "good works." Both bitterly opposed the Church sale of indulgences, collection of tithes and ownership of land. Both sought to close the monasteries and convents, abolish the office of clergy and break completely with the pope.

But although the two reformers were one in their opposition to the Church, they were in marked disagreement on other matters. With respect to religion, Luther had maintained that faith alone was sufficient to assure a man of salvation, while Calvin stated that God had so ordained for some people to be saved and others to be damned, and that neither faith nor "good works" could help one who was facing damnation.

However, it was in the realm of social thought that the two men differed most significantly. Luther supported the institution of monarchy; Calvin was against it. Luther regarded a titled aristocracy as being necessary to a society;

Calvin considered a person to be noble only if he was in God's favor. Luther had the medieval churchman's and peasant's prejudice against profit obtained through trade; Calvin sanctioned it; in fact, he thought the income of the merchant to be essentially more honest than that of the landowner. His preference for those who became wealthy through trade, rather than through the collection of rent from the use of land, was expressed in a letter to a correspondent:

"What reason is there why the income from business should not be larger than that from landowning? Whence, do the merchant's profits come, except from his own diligence and industry?"[6]

Calvin also went so far as to approve of money lending, or usury, at least among the wealthy:

"Those who think differently, may object, that we must abide by God's judgment when He generally prohibits all usury to His people. I reply, that the question is only as to the poor, and consequently, if we have to do with the rich that usury is freely permitted; because the Lawgiver, in alluding to one thing, seems not to condemn another concerning which God is silent. If again they object that usurers are absolutely condemned by David and Ezekiel, I think that their declarations ought to be judged of by the role of charity; and therefore that only those unjust exactions are condemned whereby the creditor, losing sight of equity, burdens and oppresses his debtor."[7]

Thus, Calvin approved of investing as well as of trading, both economic activities being so essential to the growth of capitalism. It is significant that he also condemned idleness which would interfere with capitalistic development. If fact, Calvin and his ministers preached that if one was diligent and industrious and prospered therefrom, he was

6. Quoted from Richard H. Tawney, *Religion and the Rise of Capitalism*, London, 1927, p. 105.
7. Calvin, *Commentaries on the Four Last Books of Moses*, trans. Rev. Charles W. Bingham, Exodus 22: 25, Edinburgh, 1854.

giving ample proof of being in God's favor. By his very actions he was showing that he was to be saved.

The question now arises as to why Luther and Calvin stressed different themes. Why, in particular, was the one an ardent nationalist and the other a true exponent of capitalistic enterprise? Because, aside from their contrasting personal backgrounds, the circumstances of their respective countries—Germany and France—were so different.

Germany, in the sixteenth century, was not a nation in the sense that France was. She had neither a king, in the true sense, nor a court, nor a capital. She was without a rallying point or a nucleus around which to establish a national life. How had such a failure come about? Simply because in Germany, in contrast to France, England, and Spain there had been no opportunity for the kings or emperors to cooperate with a burgher class in controlling the dukes, counts, and barons. The Holy Roman emperors had appeared on the historical scene far too early to be of assistance to or receive help from a thriving merchant class. The Holy Roman Empire had been proclaimed in 962; the burghers in Germany, like the bourgeoisie elsewhere in Europe, did not really become prominent until the twelfth century, but by then the German emperors, unlike the kings of England and France, were losing their hold on the country. In effect, it could be said that Germany was a victim of premature expansion, premature because the period of empire building, and of consequent monarchial growth, had occurred far too early in her history. And owing to this fact, and to the failure to become a nation, nationalism was stirring in the Germany of Luther's day.

What, on the other hand, were the circumstances in France? There, the kings, with the assistance of the bourgeoisie, had virtually succeeded in uniting the country; indeed, they were becoming absolute monarchs. To be sure, there were, in the sixteenth century, plots and intrigues at court and insurrections and religious conflicts in the outlying provinces; the kings, however, had the upper hand. In the France of Calvin's day, the question was not one of trying to establish but rather of attempting to curtail the royal power. Those most interested in controlling the king were the lesser nobles and the bourgeoisie, particularly those who were in the legal profession. Such were the very classes and occupation to which Calvin's family belonged.

On their part, the French bourgeoisie of the sixteenth century were neither as prosperous nor as prominent in their respective communities as were their German contemporaries. In France there weren't any great banking families that could compare with the Fuggers and Welsers of Augsburg. The French capitalists were just beginning to assert themselves; theirs was an uphill struggle, and it was this struggle which was reflected in the Calvinistic doctrines. Hence, it is not surprising that Calvin, more than Luther, harbored the urban middle-class hostility to the Church and even went beyond the German reformer in trying to prove the uselessness of the Catholic clergy.

Calvin's doctrines were readily accepted in just those societies where the bourgeoisie and lesser seigneurs were resisting the rise of absolute monarchy. They were most enthusiastically received by those who disputed the claim of a monarch, native or foreign, to rule by divine right. Accordingly, they won converts, not only in France, but in Switzerland, the country to which Calvin fled to escape arrest by the French king's agents. For the Swiss middle classes were well aware that the Hapsburgs had not abandoned their plan to subdue the rugged Alpine republic. Calvinism had even wider appeal in sixteenth-century Holland and seventeenth-century Scotland, where the burghers were up in arms against the Spanish king, Philip II, and the Scottish king, James I, respectively, monarchs who claimed to be God's appointees for the kingship.

It was not long before Calvinism spread from Holland and Scotland to England. There, the traders, craftsmen and shopkeepers were engaged in a political struggle with King James and, subsequently, his son and successor, King Charles I, who also claimed the kingship by divine right. This royal claim might not have irritated the burgesses had not the two kings pursued a feudal economic policy which favored the leading agricultural interests—the peers and gentry. During the reign of Charles, the protests of the urban middle classes were voiced in Parliament, but the king only listened with a deaf ear. By 1628, parliamentary procedure having failed to bring about reconciliation, civil war erupted.

With the victory of the Roundheads (parliamentarians) over the Cavaliers (royalists), and the establishment of the Commonwealth under Oliver Cromwell, in 1649, Calvinism came fully to the fore. The influence of Calvin was felt in all phases of English life, political, economic and cultural, as well as religious. The kingship was swept aside, and considerations of noble rank were disregarded. Business interests were well catered to, and trade, both domestic and foreign, was promoted on a vast scale; indeed, under the Puritan regime, England become more prosperous than ever. On the other hand, all amusements and even artistic displays were forbidden. Maypole dances, dramas, and concerts were banned, as were festivals and pageants.

It was here that the ascetic side of Calvinism asserted itself. For Calvin and his followers had maintained that one should promote wealth and prosperity but not enjoy it. Enjoyment would mean that one was not practicing self-denial, and such practice was necessary to justify one's hostility to the Church. Indeed, despite their differences, the Calvinists and the Lutherans had this in common: they considered it very necessary to undergo severe tests and adhere strictly to the Word. In this way they could prove their moral superiority to the Catholics; herein, they could demonstrate that they were more priestlike than the priests, whom they had ousted. Concerning the benefits of experiencing tribulation, Luther wrote to a friend:

"Wait upon the Lord! Be of good cheer! Were there no such thing as tribulation to try Christian faith, what would become of secure, indolent, self-indulgent Christians? Surely the same as has befallen the papacy. Inasmuch as tribulation serves the same purpose as rhubarb, myrrh, aloes, or an antidote against all the worms, poison, decay and dung of this body of death, it ought not to be despised. We must not willfully seek or select afflictions, but we must accept those which God sees fit to visit upon us, for He knows which are suitable and salutary for us and how many and how heavy they should be."[8]

A comparable attempt to furnish moral ground for the Reformation was put forth by Calvin in a letter to the Duke of Somerset, Lord Protector of England, during the reign of King Edward VI (r. 1547-1553) :

"It is evident that the Christianity of the Papacy is spurious and counterfiet, and it will be condemned in the judgment of God at the last day, as it is so manifestly repugnant to His word. If it is your intention to withdraw the people from this gulph, you must follow the example of the Apostle. In treating of the restoration of the Lord's Supper to its proper use, he enjoins them to be united in removing those additions which had crept in among them: 'I have received,' he says, 'of the Lord that which, also, I deliver unto you . . .' Hence, we may deduce this general principle, that when we enter upon a lawful reformation, which may be acceptable to God, we must adhere to His pure and uncorrupted word; for all those mixtures, engendered in the human mind which remain, will be so many manifest pollutions, tending to withdraw men from

---

8. Luther, "Letter to Anthony Lauterbach," in *Letters of Spiritual Counsel, Library of Christian Classics*, Vol. XVIII.

the right use of those things, which He hath instituted for their salvation."[9]

To the Calvinists and Lutherans alike, adherence to the Word came to mean the performance of one's duty to society. However, the followers of Calvin, alone, believed the ideal society to be one which is free from royal absolutism and wholly encouraging to business enterprise.

During the era of the English Civil War and the Commonwealth (1629-1660), Calvinism, or Puritanism, became thoroughly ingrained in the English as well as Scottish way of life. Ever since the advent of the Restoration, in 1660, the British people have been, in large measure, republican, and this despite their devotion to the royal family. Indeed, one reason that monarchy has endured so long among the British is its strict constitutionality. The same could be said for the aristocracy. For one thing, almost all of the feudal noble families had disappeared during the War of the Roses (1453-1485), so that the aristocrats of the seventeenth century were descendants of merchants and squires. Then too, while retaining their estates and titles, the British peers have wholeheartedly engaged in business and become pioneers of capitalism. Finally, Britons, of all classes, have practiced thrift and austerity, more from habit than from necessity. In this, they seemed to have also taken heed of the words of John Milton who, on the occasion of the Roundhead victory in the Civil War, wrote:

"Unless you expel avarice, ambition and luxury from your minds, yes, and extravagance from your families as well, you will find at home and within that tyrant who, you believed, was to be sought abroad and in the field— now even more stubborn. In fact, many tyrants, impossible to endure, will, from day to day, hatch out from your very vitals. Conquer them first. This is the warfare of peace,

9. Calvin, *Memoirs of the Life and Writings*, comp. Rev. Elijah Waterman, Hartford, 1813, p. 338.

these are its victories, hard indeed, but bloodless and far more noble than the gory victories of war. Unless you be victors here as well, that enemy and tyrant whom you have just now defeated in the field has either not been conquered at all or has been conquered in vain."[10]

Republicanism, individualistic capitalistic enterprise, and frugality—these characteristics have been evident everywhere that Calvinism achieved a victory. Accordingly, they have been apparent in Switzerland, Holland and New England, as well as in Scotland and Old England.

From these countries the Calvinistic doctrines were transplanted back to France, though the majority of French people remained Catholic. Yet, once implanted in the French soil, they helped to nourish the seeds for the Revolution of 1789. For as the Calvinists condemned all those who were idle, so did the French political theorists scorn the nobles who, in France, contributed so little to society.

Still, the distance from Calvinism to Jacobinism was formidable. The Calvinists stressed the duty and, like other Christians, the sinfulness of man; the Jacobins, his dignity and nobility. Although the Calvinists encouraged the common man to overthrow the king and rid himself of the idle peer, it was in order that he could be diligent and ascetic, promote business and thus prove that he is in the grace of God.

Before the western Europeans could look upon man as being essentially noble, in the sight of God, instead of sinful, they had to become even less otherworldly and be concerned solely with the present world. This change in perspective could come about only through the influence of Humanism and the Enlightenment. But before many Europeans could become Humanistic and "Enlightened," a second phase of interaction, in modern times, was necessary.

---

10. Milton, "A Second Defense of the English People," from *Complete Prose Works*, New Haven, 1966, Vol. IV, Pt. I.

C. The Interactive Assault on the Semi-Feudal State: The Renaissance, Enlightenment, French Revolution and Self-Gratification

When the waves of interaction swept against the Church, they caused the birth of medieval and modern Protestantism. When they beat against the semi-feudal State, they gave rise to Humanism, the Enlightenment, and the French Revolution. But the psychological tendencies which formed the basis of Humanism and the Enlightenment differed considerably from those which accompanied the growth of Protestantism.

We saw that the waves of interaction had brought to shore a prominent bourgeoisie. We saw further that this new class was resentful toward feudal society. Ironically enough, many of the bourgeoisie could harbor feelings of resentment because, with their gradual accumulation of wealth, they had sufficient time and leisure to think.

Leisure, however, brought forth still another fruitful result. It led to a deep interest in study, particularly in a study of the classics. Interest in the classics had been aroused by the Church itself, and especially by such renowned Scholastics as Albertus Magnus (1193-1247) and St. Thomas Aquinas (1225-1274), with their translations of Aristotle.

But in delving into the classics, in becoming Humanists, the middle class scholars became interested in more than a mere knowledge of the works of antiquity. They soon wished to imitate the Greeks and Romans—acquire their joy of living and this worldly perspective. In so doing, these learned men of the late Middle Ages became far less concerned with Christian thought—with the Doctrine of Original Sin, ideas of the soul and the hereafter. They became more interested in knowledge than in salvation, curious about their own world and less obsessed with the future of their souls. Thus, the Italian Humanist, Francesca Petrarca (Petrarch) (1304-1374), was led to imagine the following dialogue between himself and St. Augustine:

"I will be true to myself, in so far as in me lies. But even while we speak, a crowd of important affairs, though only of the world, is awaiting my attention. I am not ignorant that as you, St. Augustine, said, a few minutes before, it would be much safer for me to attend to the cares of my soul, to relinquish altogether every bypath and follow the straight path of the way to salvation. But I have not the strength to resist that old bent for study altogether."[11]

The century and a half following the age of Petrarch saw a steadily mounting interest in the present world. These hundred and fifty years saw the full flowering of the Renaissance spirit. They saw the voyages of Columbus, Magellan, and Vasco da Gama, as well as the artistic creations of Da Vinci, Raphael, and Michelangelo. They saw the introduction of the mariner's compass, the devising of accounting and banking systems and the invention of the printing press. These voyages and innovations marked the beginning of a second wave of interaction in western Europe, the wave known in economic history as the Commercial Revolution. But they did more. They broadened man's perspective and made many individuals actually indifferent to ideas of sin and salvation. Hence, it was not long before an apology for mere study expressed by a Petrarch gave way to an open ridicule of asceticism and excessive piety. Such scorn for piety and asceticism prompted the Dutch Humanist, Desiderius Erasmus (1466-1536), to write:

"The Christian religion, on the whole, seems to have a kinship with some sort of folly, while it has no alliance whatever with wisdom. If you want proof of this statement, observe, first of all, how children, old people, women

---

1. *Petrarch's Secret*, trans. W. H. Draper, London, 1911, pp. 191-92.

and fools find pleasure beyond other folk in holy and religious things and to that end are ever nearest the altars, led, no doubt, solely by an impulse of nature. Then you will notice that the original founders of religion, admirably laying hold of pure simplicity, were the bitterest foes of literary learning. Lastly, no fools seem to act more foolishly than do the people whom zeal for Christian piety has got possession of, for they pour out their wealth, they overlook wrongs, allow themselves to be cheated, make no distinction between friends and enemies, shun pleasure, glut themselves with hunger, wakefulness, tears, toils and reproaches; they disdain life and dearly prefer death; in short, they seem to have grown utterly numb to ordinary sensations, quite as if their souls lived elsewhere and not in their bodies. What is this, forsooth, but to be mad?"[12]

Erasmus corresponded frequently with Luther, but the two men generally disagreed. One emphasized the duty, the other, the dignity of man; Luther told man to be humble, while Erasmus urged him to be dignified and rational. Already, we can see the discrepancy between Protestantism and Humanism, between the spirit of the Reformation and that of the Renaissance.

The spirit of the Renaissance soon spread from Holland to France, where it appeared in the writings of Francois Rabelais (1490-1553) and Michel de Montaigne (1533-1592). Rabelais, like Erasmus, mocked the excessive piety and asceticism in his day and, though less forceful in his criticism, was nevertheless influential. Montaigne, a descendant of a Gascon wine merchant, retired in later life to his estate to study himself. It was during this time that he composed his *Essais*. In these writings, he too displayed a thinly veiled contempt for medieval religious morality and for those who are so pious that they forsake all pleasure. He wrote:

---

12. Erasmus, *The Praise of Folly*, trans. Hoyt Hopewell Hudson, Princeton, 1941, p. 118.

"Be pleased here to excuse what I often repeat, that I very rarely repent, and that my conscience is satisfied with itself, not as the conscience of an angel, or that of a horse, but as the conscience of a man.

"In my opinion, 'tis the happy living, and not (as Antisthenes said) the happy dying, in which human felicity consists . . . Were I to live my life over again, I should live it just as I have lived it; I neither complain of the past, nor do I fear the future, and if I am not much deceived, I am the same within that I am without. 'Tis one main obligation I have to my fortune that the succession of my bodily estate has been carried on according to the natural seasons; I have seen the grass, the blossom and the fruit, and now see the withering; happily, however, because naturally."[13]

So far, we have seen the Renaissance appear in Italy, Holland and France. For since it was inspired by an interflow of knowledge, it could flourish only in certain societies: those which had aristocracies and, even more important, urban middle classes whose members were exposed to new ideas and had ample leisure to study and evaluate them. Such was the occasion in the Italy of Petrarch's day, the Holland of Erasmus's, and the France of Rabelais's and Montaigne's. From these three countries the light of the Renaissance was carried to Spain and England. In Spain it endured long enough to produce the *Don Quixote* of Miguel de Cervantes, until extinguished by the Inquisition. In England, on the contrary, it continued to shine; here, its reflection could be seen in the literature of the Elizabethan Age (1558-1603). In the England of the seventeenth century, however, it was dimmed by the somber Puritan atmosphere. Although the rays from the Renaissance did glow again in the eighteenth

---

13. Montaigne, "Of Repentance," from *The Essays,* Charles Cotton's trans., ed. C. Carew Haslitt (Bohn) in *Great Books of the World,* London, 1952, Vol. 25.

century, when they even appeared as the Enlightenment, Puritanism yet lingered in the background.

The coexistence of Humanism and Puritanism was evident in the British literature of the eighteenth century. Among the numerous authors there were two who were quite realistic in their appraisal of man and did not bewail the fact that he was occasionally "amoral." In *Roxana,* Daniel Defoe tried to show how individuals in love do at times have illicit relationships; in *Tom Jones,* Henry Fielding portrayed even "respectable" persons as succumbing to desire; both authors were quite objective on this question.

Before writing his famed work, Fielding had been irritated by the prudishness of Samuel Richardson who, in *Pamela,* gave undue stress to the desirability of having a woman conform to the set standards. But Richardson was not alone in his taste for Puritan morality. Joseph Addison, Richard Steele, and Jonathan Swift also directed their satire toward nonconformity. And, significantly, Samuel Johnson, the arbiter of the then British literary world, harbored the opinions of the Puritan pastors when writing as follows about mankind:

"The depravity of mankind is so easily discoverable that nothing but the desert or the call can exclude it from notice. The knowledge of crimes intrudes uncalled and undesired. They whom their abstraction from common occurrences hinders him from seeing iniquity will quickly have their attention awakened by feeling it. Even he who ventures not into the world may learn its corruption in his closet. For what are treatises of morality but persuasives to the practice of duties for which no argument would be necessary but that we are continually tempted to violate or neglect them? What are all the records of history but narratives of successive villainies, of treason and usurpations, massacres and wars?"[14]

---

14. Johnson, "The Majority are Wicked," in *The Rambler* (Everyman) 1953.

Judging from the above passage, it is not surprising that Johnson also wrote forcefully about the need for repentance and self-denial:

"Austerities and mortifications are means by which the mind is invigorated and roused, by which the attractions of pleasure are interrupted, and the chains of sensuality are broken. It is observed by one of the fathers that he who restrains himself in the use of things lawful, will never encroach upon things forbidden ... Austerity is the proper antidote to indulgence. The diseases of the mind as well as body are cured by contraries, and to contraries we should readily have recourse, if we dreaded guilt as we dread pain."[15]

In these passages the somber Puritan atmosphere is all too evident.

Rather than to England in the Age of Johnson we must turn to France to seek a society where the Enlightenment shined most brilliantly. For here, all the factors were present to make such an illumination possible. With her abundance of fertile soil, France was able to sustain a population which was much larger than that of England. Moreover, with her exposure to the Mediterranean, as well as to the Atlantic, she not only engaged in lucrative trade and experienced the rise of a wealthy bourgeoisie. She also was more receptive to the mood of the Renaissance, which had arisen in the South, while having avoided the rigors of the Reformation in the North. Owing to these favorable circumstances, and to the fact that France, like England, was a consolidated state, the French bourgeoisie were most imbued with the new Enlightenment.

Hence, it was in eighteenth-century France that the Renaissance spirit of tolerance toward man was furthered. Furthermore, alongside the belief that natural desire is healthful and wholesome, there arose the view that man is an essentially noble rather than sinful being. Indeed, the idea that he is an inherently good instead of evil creature

5. *Ibid.*, "Repentance."

served as a justification for enjoying pleasures, in moderation of course, without the all too frequently added feelings of guilt.

In the furtherance of these twin concepts, the French
writers far surpassed the British. Admittedly, there were
two British political theorists—John Locke and Jeremy
Bentham—who were more tolerant of man than were most
of their fellow countrymen. Locke considered man to be
at least reasonable enough to warrant popular government,
while Bentham, though regarding him as self-seeking,
stated that his selfishness is for the good of society. Still,
the French "philosophes" were more generous in their
appraisal of the human race.

In the following passage, Voltaire maintained that there
is a reasonable basis for believing that man is born virtuous:

"We are perpetually told that human nature is essentially perverse, that man is born a child of the devil. Now
nothing can be more imprudent; for my friend, in preaching to me that all the world is born in wickedness, thou
informest me that thou are born so, and that behooves me
to beware of thee as I would of a fox or a crocodile . .
Much more rational and much more handsome would i
be to say to men, 'You are all born good, consider how
dreadful it would be to defile the purity of your being.
Mankind should be dealt with as individuals. If a preb
endary leads a scandalous life, a friend says to him, 'Is i
possible that you can thus disgrace the dignity of a preb
endary?' A counsellor or judge is reminded that he ha
the honour of being counsellor to the king; and that it i
his duty to be an example of virtue. The encouragemen
to a soldier is, 'Remember you belong to the regiment c
Champaigne'; and every individual should be told, 'R
member your dignity as a man.' "[16]

_____

16. Voltaire, "Wicked, Wickedness," in *The Philosophical Dictionar*
London, Jacques & Co., 1802.

Even more compassionate was Jean Jacques Rousseau, who stated frankly that man is inherently noble, a nobility which is indicated by his sense of sympathy:

"Let us not conclude, with [Thomas] Hobbes, that because man has no idea of goodness, he must be naturally wicked . . . that he always refuses to do his fellow creatures services which he does not think they have a right to demand; or that by virtue of the right he truly claims to everything he needs, he foolishly imagines himself the sole proprietor of the universe . . . There is another principle which has escaped Hobbes; which having been bestowed on mankind, to moderate, on certain occasions, the impetuosity of egoism, or before its birth, the desire of self-preservation, tempers the ardour with which he pursues his own welfare, by an innate repugnance at seeing a fellow-creature suffer."[17]

Such sentiment was consistent with that which Rousseau expressed in other passages from the same work: that the common man had been just and noble until corrupted by the wealth, greed, and vanity of civilization.

Rousseau's writings, in particular, were received with wide acclaim by the reading public. For in contending that man is noble, but that his inherent goodness had been marred by the avarice and corruption of an aristocratic social order, he struck a tender note. Already, the claim of the nobles and higher clergy that they merited their exalted status in society was being viewed with skepticism. Now, they could be held responsible for the corruption which, hitherto, had been regarded as inherent in man.

In fact, Rousseau, Voltaire, lesser "philosophes" and earlier Humanists helped to remove from the common people the feeling of guilt and quest for repentance which had been fostered by tradition. Since their historical guilt

7. Rousseau, "A Dissertation on the Origin and Foundation of the Inequality of Mankind," in *The Social Contract and Discourses* (Everyman), 1946.

feeling was considerably lessened, those who led and participated in the French Revolution did not need to feel as priestly as the priest was supposed to feel, or be as humble as did those who had taken part in the Reformation. It is largely for this reason that the French Revolution, and its ideology, were more extreme than were the English Puritan Revolution and its social philosophy. In England, the idea that man should, in some way, redeem himself led even the most liberal thinkers to hold to the Puritan view that only those who create wealth are to be highly esteemed. Therefore, they thought, as long as the aristocracy promotes capitalistic growth and prosperity, it may retain its titles and privileges. In France, however, where such a need for redemption was not considered necessary, the *philosophes* stated that all men have equal rights and are worthy of consideration. Whereas the English Puritan and Glorious Revolutions had entailed only the institution of liberty against an arbitrary sovereign, the "deluge" in France was such as to sweep away all remnants of manorialism and aristocratic prerogative. By the close of the Napoleonic Era, France, like Britain much earlier, had passed from the expansive to the interactive stage. But the French passage was more complete.

D. Major Expansive and Interactive Societies in Europe: A Study in Similarity and Contrast

In the preceding chapter, we observed that the great upheaval of 1789 enabled the French society to become more interactive than the British. However, a view of Europe, in the nineteenth century, would reveal an even wider range of differences among societies than those between France and Great Britain. For aside from these two states, there are three other major societies—Italy, German and Russia—to consider. Of the five, Russia, Germany and

Italy remained in the expansive stage of history, while Great Britain and France had entered the interactive. But before comparing and contrasting them, let us review briefly the characteristics of the one group as opposed to the other.

Expansive and interactive societies may be said to differ in three ways. They are discrepant in regard to their political systems, social structures and social and religious thought or philosophy.

In our survey of the ancient world, we noted that expansive societies were inevitably ruled by either hereditary monarchs or (for a period in Rome and China) by dictatorgenerals. Alongside this centralization of authority was the rise of a privileged military nobility. The autocracy and aristocracy had not only emerged as a result of expansion, but they, in turn, promoted imperialism, since their exalted status depended upon military victory. In contrast, the interactive societies were governed by legislative bodies representing mainly business interests. These bodies brooked little or no interference from kings or aristocracies, because it would only jeopardize interaction.

We may further note that social and religious thought differed from the one type of society to the other. In the interactive, there were philosophers, such as Thales, who were skeptical of traditional religious beliefs; there were scholars, like Aristotle, who ridiculed outdated institutions; and there were playwrights, like Euripides, who protested the mistreatment of vanquished enemies. But while protesting and showing skepticism, they had no desire to change drastically or escape from the society itself. As long as the society in which they lived was interactive, they merely wished to reform it.

In the expansive states, on the contrary, poets, prose writers and historians presented different themes. There were some who defended the martial spirit which had rendered the imperialism possible. In Rome, Horace and

Livy referred to the Spartan-like virtues of their earlier countrymen and longed for their revival. There were others, however, who spoke in glowing terms of the conquests and of the glory which they brought to their state and then regretted having championed such military exploits. Thus, Vergil wrote in his *Aeneid* of how the Romans were to become a great race, and later, in the *Georgics,* he protested the excesses of the legionnaires. Similarly, in the Byzantine empire, the historian Procopius praised the deeds of the Emperor Justinian; but later, in his *Secret History,* he condemned this avaricious ruler and his general, Belisaurius. The tendency of literati, in an expansive society, to be strongly for or against the existing order was due largely, of course, to their feeling of guilt, or lack of it, over the conquest and exploitation of others. But then, an added factor was the rigid and warlike nature of the society itself, and the alternative of either being identified with or feeling alienated from the ruling hierarchy.

Indeed, there were occasions, in ancient and medieval times, in which the society was expansive, but certain of its communities were migratory. Earliest illustrations were the mystery societies and cults, which had arisen in Greece and the Orient, and flourished in the Roman empire. Later examples were the monastic orders—the Benedictines, Cistercians and Carthusians—founded in Europe prior to the Urban Revolution. These veritable societies within a society were interested in promoting bonds of unity among their members, even if doing so entailed collectivization of their economy. Still further examples could be found during the Bohemian and German Reformations, when groups of peasants and artisans broke with the mainstream of Protestants and advocated communism. For in their urgent desire to form cohesive and binding units, they sought the removal of all alleged barriers to unity, economic as well as social and religious. The abolition of private property, they thought, would fulfill such a purpose. In Bohemia, the peasants and artisans formed the radical wing of the Hussite movement and were known as Taborites. In Germany, they severed relations with the Lutherans and referred to themselves as Anabaptists, since they believed that baptism should be administered only to converted adults rather than to children. Though having failed as a movement in central Europe, Anabaptism, with its evangelism and communism, spread eastward to societies where circumstances were such as to encourage it.

One such society was Russia. For here, the political and social system was expansive, but the communities themselves were, in a sense, already migratory. Here too, as we shall note, the expansive structure was particularly oppressive, so much so as to gradually create a wide gulf between the ruling hierarchy and the mass of subjects.

At the time that its era of expansion had commenced, Russian society was still under the tutelage of the Tatars. But it was the very rule of the Tatars which rendered expansion possible. For in the fourteenth century, Ivan Kalita, Grand Duke of Moscow, secured the privilege of collecting taxes for the Tatar khans, and with the grant of this privilege went the premission to control the policies of neighboring princes. This practice was continued under Kalita's successors, Vasili II and Ivan the Great, the latter having defeated the Mongols themselves in 1480, thus breaking the Tatar yoke. Ivan the Great also married a princess from Byzantium and, in so doing, introduced all the ceremonial, pomp, and regal splendor of the Byzantine court.

During this period of initial expansion, Russian society was roughly divided into four classes. Uppermost were the Votshina, or hereditary landowners, whose ancestors had rendered valuable assistance to the Slavic princes in subjugating the surrounding territory. The Votshina, known also as boyars, bequeathed their estates to their sons from generation to generation. Below them were a newer class, the Pomietsche, or conditional landowners, whose tenure was maintained as long as they continued to render military service. The mass of subjects were Smerdy, or peasants, who still were permitted to change their abode as they saw fit, while at the bottom of the social scale were the Kholopi, or slaves. At one time, there had been a class of merchants, but they disappeared with the Tatar invasion.

As the Russian state continued to expand, throughout the sixteenth, seventeenth, and eighteenth centuries, and encompass White Russian, Ukranian, and Tatar lands, its social structure was changed to meet the needs of an empire. The boyars, long regarded by the grand dukes and subsequent tsars as unreliable in times of trouble, were gradually liquidated, while the class of military landowners, or gentry, was enlarged until during the reign of Peter the Great (r. 1696-1725) it comprised a veritable army.

Since the gentry were subject to call on short notice, they had to have some means of economic support. Hence, even as early as the sixteenth century, the tsars issued decrees conscripting peasants to work on the estates of squires who needed help, the rulers also forbid them to leave these manors. From the sixteenth century on, the condition of the Russian peasants grew from bad to worse. The proportion of servile tenants became even larger until under Peter the Great those who had managed to remain free were enserfed to provide farm labor for the numerous military proprietors.

Serfdom had also been widely introduced in other eastern European countries, even while it was disappearing in western Europe. But in Russia this institution was more oppressive than it was elsewhere. A Russian squire could demand from his serf any kind of heavy work, whether it was in the fields, the manorial workshop or the mansion.

For a slight or even imagined display of effrontery he could have a serf knouted; for disobedience he could have him banished to Siberia. If feeling lustful, he might violate a female serf, and some country gentlemen were known to keep harems.[18] Against such abuses and violations the serfs received little or no protection from the government. For the administrators themselves were appointed from the gentry, and they did the utmost to safeguard the privileges of their class.

How did the Russian peasant react to this oppression? First, he escaped, usually to the steppes or to the region of the Caucasus. Then later, when it appeared as though such means of refuge were barred, he resorted to rebellion.

As early as the fourteenth century, Russian peasants had migrated to the Don and Volga river basins. At that time, they were seeking refuge from a farm tenancy system in which the boyars demanded exorbitant dues and fees as the price of tilling a plot of earth. In their new homes, the colonists, known subsequently as Cossacks, reverted to the early Slavic migratory pattern. They established independent tribal republics, presided over by atamans, or chieftains, who were elected by village assemblies. They arranged for each of their communities to be self-sufficient units. They set up a communal land system, declaring that all property, with the exception of dwellings, belonged to the villages.

Why did they revert to the custom of communal land ownership instead of introducing private property? Because such collectivization was traditional. In the Slavic communities, from earliest times, it was the village elders who were entrusted with the supervision and distribution of land.[19] Since the Cossacks were tribal-minded peasants from an inland region rather than independent and enter-

18. Jerome Blum, *Lord and Peasant in Russia from the Ninth to the Nineteenth Century,* Princeton, 1961, p. 437.
19. Bernard Pares, *A History of Russia,* London, 1949, p. 151.

prising merchants from coastal areas, this communal land system appeared to them to be most natural. In effect, it gave them a sense of belonging.

During the fifteenth century, these Cossack republics only grudgingly acknowledged the overlordship of the Moscow grand dukes; in the seventeenth, they attracted thousands of peasants who were anxious to escape the restrictions imposed by the tsar. In the seventeenth and eighteenth, with the continued expansion of the Russian state, and the movement of the gentry to the southeast, the Cossacks and refugee peasants, fearful of becoming enserfed, took up arms against the tsar and the squires. These uprisings shook the Russian social edifice to its foundations. For under such influential leaders as Ivan Bolotnikov (c. 1610), Stenka Razin (c. 1660), and Emeliel Pugachev (c. 1770), the Cossacks, refugee peasants and also runaway slaves ravaged the countryside, burning fields and manor houses. Forcing the squires to flee, they urged their serfs to join in the rebellions, and many of them did.

These uprisings were suppressed and their leaders executed. But they awakened in the peasants throughout Russia a deeply rooted desire to do away with the manorial system. In its place they would restore the land to the mirs, or village communities. For all along, the peasants had been convinced that the land was the mir's by natural right.

It was their belief that temporally the earth belonged to the mirs and spiritually to God. For religion, too, entered fully into the agrarian struggle. In fact, Christianity was a source of inspiration for later peasant rebellions. The Christian creeds which appealed to the rebels were the Taborite and Anabaptist.

Peasant uprisings continued well into the nineteenth century, though they were not on as large a scale as before. But the grievances of the rural dwellers, together with the attachment they had to the mir, profoundly influenced literary expression. Indeed, some of the literati had such deep sympathies for the peasant that they idealized early Slavic institutions. In coming forth as the exponents of Slavism, the writers identified the expansive hierarchy with foreign culture—the bureaucracy with Prussianism and the French-speaking gentry with Westernism. To be sure, Russian writers were, to an extent, imbued with French Revolutionary or German romantic concepts, but still they remained Slavophil and migratory in outlook.

An early champion of the Russian "people" as against the upper class was Alexander Pushkin. This earliest of Russian literary figures believed that those who are ambitious and strive to rise above the masses will suffer in the end. For ambition leads to selfishness, and since selfishness is contrary to the popular will, the egotist will perish. This was the theme in his short stories and also in his epic drama, *Boris Godunov*. Aside from extolling the masses, Pushkin also wrote of the "sacred" soil of Russia.

An even firmer believer in the sanctity and purity of Slavic institutions was Alexander Herzen (1812-1870). To Herzen the *mir* was the sanctuary of the Russian people against all baneful foreign influences. While having been sufficiently exposed to French Revolutionary doctrine to favor individual freedom in a society, Herzen, nevertheless, referred to the communal village as the hope of Russia. He wrote:

"The commune saved the Russian people from Mongolian barbarism and from imperial civilization, from the gentry with its European veneer, and from the German bureaucracy. Communal organization, though strongly saken, withstood the interference of the state; it survived fortunately until the development of socialism in Europe.

"The peasant has preserved only his insignificant modest commune; i.e., the possession in common of the land, the equality of all members of the commune without exception, the fraternal division of the fields according to the number of workers, and the autonomous direction by the commune of its affairs."[20]

Herzen was only better known than two other theorists of like mind: Konstantin Askakov (1817-1860) and Alexei Khomiakov (1804-1861), both of whom had equally migratory perspectives. Askakov contended that by living in a commune the individual loses his vanity; this loss constitutes a triumph for the human spirit. Khomiakov maintained that the Eastern, or Orthodox, Church, with its atmosphere of brotherhood, is the only true Church.

Most renowned of all Russian Slavophils was Feodor Dostoevsky. For in the manner of a Hebrew patriarch when speaking of early Judaism, Dostoevsky considered the God worshipped in Russia to be the sole God that can help humanity. Russia, with her peasantry and Orthodoxy, was the abode of Christian purity and Moscow, the true Rome! In his novel *The Possessed*, he has the character Shatov say:

"Every people is only a people so long as it has its own god and excludes all other gods on earth irreconcilably; so long as it believes that by its god it will conquer and drive out of the world all other gods. . . . If a great people does not believe that the truth is only to be found in itself alone and in it exclusively; if it does not believe that it alone is fit and destined to raise up and save all the rest by its truth, it would at once sink into being ethnographical material, and not a great people. . . . But there is only one truth, and therefore only a single one out of the nations can have the true God, even though other nations may have great gods of their own. Only one nation is god-bearing; that's the Russian people."[21]

Thus, Dostoevsky was a staunch believer in Russia's

20. Martin E. Malio, "Herzen and the Peasant Commune," in *Continuity and Change in Russian and Soviet Thought*, ed. E. J. Simmons, Cambridge, Mass., Harvard University Press, 1955.
21. Dostoevsky, *The Possessed*, trans. C. Garnett, London, 1914; New York, 1960; Pt. II, Ch. I, VII.

"holy mission" to restore the spiritual life of man. Also, in the "Unveiling of the Pushkin Memorial," he yearned for a brotherhood of the European, or Aryan, people, but such, he thought, could come about only if Europe would receive the message which Russia can give her.

Russia's other leading novelist, Leo Tolstoi, was likewise a Slavophil; he, too, believed that his country alone had the solution to Europe's woes. Indeed, Tolstoi's only point of departure from Dostoevsky was his severe denunciation of the expansive society in its entirety, Russian as well as foreign. He vehemently attacked the wars and the armaments race, and, to him, the overthrow of contemporary governments seemed to be the answer to the violence ever pending in his day.[22] In certain respects, his ideas resembled those of the Marxian socialists, for he also looked upon private property as a basic evil and would abolish it. In *The End of the Age* he says:

"Senseless and ruinous armaments and wars and the deprivation of the people of their common right to the land—these, in my opinion, are the causes of the revolution impending over the whole of Christendom. And this revolution is beginning in no other place but in Russia, because nowhere except amongst the Russian people has the Christian way of life been preserved in such strength and purity and nowhere save in Russia has been so far conserved the agricultural condition of the majority of the people."[23]

In effect, Tolstoi represented the more militant phase of the migratory culture in Russia. And it was this phase which led to the gigantic upheaval that was to come later.

Why, we may ask, was the migratory tradition so deeply rooted in the cultural soil of Russia? One answer is the vast Russian frontier, where local affinities and traditional

---

22. Tolstoi, "Patriotism and Government," in *Essays and Letters*, trans. A. Maude, Oxford, 1911.
23. Tolstoi, *The End of the Age*, trans. V. Tchertkoff and I. F. Mayo, London, 1906, p. 45.

Slavic institutions were kept alive. The other is the isolation from the interactive currents which, in late medieval and early modern times, had flown from the Mediterranean to the North Sea, and along the Rhine, Seine, and Thames. These currents had given rise to burgher communities, private property ownership and more individualism than existed on the Eastern frontier. Admittedly, a few small currents had been carried along the Danube and had found their way into the Black and Baltic sea areas. But the Hungarian and Polish plains and, even more, the Russian steppes and forests were too vast for them to create much of a stir and influence events in these inland regions. Consequently, Russia, in particular, was little affected by them. Hence, she failed to experience a Protestant Reformation, a Renaissance and an Enlightenment. Hence, her people lacked both the Puritan sense of duty to State or to industry and the bourgeois sophistication, so common further west. Russia's culture was, in essence, a folk culture.

When leaving Russia, in the late nineteenth century, and traveling to the societies in central and western Europe, we see far less of the migratory trend. Instead, we observe the impact of either the Reformation or the Renaissance, noting that the former has influenced Germany and Great Britain, the latter, Italy and France. Equally important, we become aware that Germany and Italy have remained in the expansive stage of history, while Great Britain and France have entered the interactive.

Crossing the Russian Polish border into Germany, we are impressed with the greater strength and integration of the German state. The source of German strength was, of course, the heavy industrialization. Such phenomenal industrial progress had a precedent. In late medieval times, when the tides of interaction swept the Rhine valley and the shores of the North and Baltic seas, they gave rise to burgher communities, with their *rats,* or town councils, *hansa,* or guilds, and atmosphere of order and diligence. It was this sense of order and application of skill which rendered possible efficient organization. Hence, in contrast to Russia the Prussian kingdom, which subsequently emerged, became famous for its competent civil service and the later German empire, for its industrial efficiency and institutions of higher learning.

Yet, despite its flourishing commerce and subsequent industrial and scientific progress, German society remained expansive. The reason was also historical. In our discussion of medieval Germany, I stated that in Germany, alone, the ruler and the townsmen had failed to cooperate in curbing the authority of the feudal lords. For by the time that the towns had become wealthy and powerful, the sovereign had all but ceased to exist. Accordingly, the urban communities learned to function independently of the defunct emperor, or of the territorial princes; they formed separate leagues and managed their own affairs.

This rift between the towns and the rulers affected German life for centuries to come. It caused the burghers to remain aloof from political and social questions, especially from those which concerned the country as a whole. It encouraged the intellectuals and men of letters, most of whom were town citizens, to think more about religious and philosophical issues and less about the problems facing society. It fostered idealism rather than realism.

Only with the momentous events of 1789, and the subsequent Napoleonic invasions did a tiny spark of burgher revolt begin to glow. For the urban classes had grievances against the aristocratic order. During the succeeding era of Metternich (1815-1848), the spark even ignited. Its ignition could be seen in the attempts of the German burghers and artisans to establish representative government, freedom of expression and the right of all to equal opportunity. It was apparent in their uprisings against the governments of Hesse and Hanover, in 1830, and in their setting up of republican regimes in Baden, the Rhenish Palatinate and Saxony, in 1848.

Yet, in Germany, such revolts were doomed to failure. Due to historical circumstances, the urban classes in these German states were neither as numerous nor as vigorous as their contemporaries in France. But an even more important cause of the failure, a cause which also had its roots in the soil of history, was the attitude of the Prussians. Admittedly, in the Prussian as well as in the other German states, the burghers and artisans demanded reforms; however, they were easily suppressed. For in no other state was the old order so firmly in the saddle; nowhere were the peasants in the army so obedient in quelling disturbances at the king's command. These same disciplined Prussian forces were dispatched to the other German states, and with the suppression of the uprisings the liberal tide receded.

Following unification under Prussia, what was the political and social system which prevailed throughout Germany? It was, to a great extent, the earlier Prussian, but it was applied to the new Second Reich. The German kaiser, like the earlier king of only Prussia, ruled as well as reigned; he, too, appointed a ministry and supervised the work of an extensive administration. The Second Reich, to be sure, had a more influential legislative body than did Prussia alone. While there was an upper chamber, or Bundesrat, consisting of delegates appointed from the various states of the empire, there was also a lower house, or Reichstag, elected by male suffrage. But the approval of both houses was necessary before legislation could be enacted. Then too, since the chancellor and his ministers were imperial appointees, the government was generally controlled by the class most influential with the kaiser.

What was this class? It was the Prussian Junker, or landowning military class; from this elite the majority of chancellors were appointed. For as they were the descendants of the Teutonic Knights, who had conquered Prussia, the Junkers were highly esteemed. Usually, the leading positions in the government and army were reserved for them, and in East Prussia, their possession of vast estates enabled them to virtually control the peasant villages in their districts.

To be sure, the Junkers had to share their status in society with the new class of industrial and financial barons along the Rhine and the Ruhr. For with the great strides made toward industrialization, the princes of industry and of high finance became influential in governmental circles. In fact, through their representatives in the Reichstag, they had some influence over foreign policy.

Still, it was the Junkers who had the final word with the kaiser, and more than one chancellor was asked to resign because of their disapproval. In 1894, Chancellor Count Caprivi, in an effort to increase trade with Austria-Hungary and Russia, agreed to lower the tariff on grain imports, if the other two nations would make similar concessions for German manufacturers. The treaty was concluded, and the German industrialists were pleased. But the Junker landowners were up in arms, and they soon secured Caprivi's dismissal.[24]

On a later occasion, when, due to the naval-building program, the imperial treasury was faced with a deficit, Chancellor Prince von Bulow proposed an inheritance tax. However, since the chancellor requested that the Junkers pay their share of the tax, he aroused their fury. Hence, their representatives in the Reichstag, together with those of the Catholic Church (whom he had antagonized on another question) urged the kaiser to dismiss him, and the sovereign complied.[25]

24. R. H. Fife, Jr., *The German Empire between Two Wars*, New York, 1918, p. 152.
25. F. W. Wile, *The Men around the Kaiser: The Makers of Modern Germany*, London, 1914, pp. 133–34.

Indeed, it could be said that the most powerful man in Germany was Dr. Ernst von Heydebrand, the leader of the Junker faction in both the Prussian state and German legislatures and known as the "uncrowned King of Prussia."[26] Thus, despite the rapid industrialization of Germany in the late nineteenth century, the German society, like the Russian, had a decidedly privileged aristocracy.

However, as I said before, Germany was far more integrated and unified than Russia. Indeed, the impact of Lutheranism and its doctrine that one must practice self-denial, especially for the state, can hardly be overestimated, as far as Germany was concerned. The family, the school and the churches taught that one should study and work hard for the benefit of the state and not idle away his time. Gradually, the idea that an individual should utilize every moment of his waking hours became almost an obsession. Punctuality became the keynote in German life, and all daily activity, whether at school or in the office and factory, was adapted to a fixed schedule; there was little time for leisure during studying or working hours. Even pleasures had a practical purpose. A British traveler observed that people attended the theatre, not so much for recreation as for education.[27] Sports, too, were popular, but their principal aim was bodybuilding rather than the sheer joy of participation. After strenuous exercise, the consumption of beer was a welcome pastime, but then the beerhalls and festivals for which Germany is famous were more prevalent in the Catholic South than in the Protestant North.

By contrast, in Russia, and especially among the gentry, there was much in the way of alcoholic and sexual indulgence; in fact, excesses were so common that the committing of sin and punishment of oneself were common

---

26. *Ibid.*, p. 99.
27. W. H. Dawson, *German Life in Town and Country*, London, 1901, p. 179.

themes among the Russian monks and intelligentsia. Also, the semifeudal society of Russia had little concern with widespread education or with punctuality, though industrialization had already begun. The mass of Russian peasants and small number of factory hands did work hard, but inefficiently.

Germany, being far less inland than Russia, and economically advanced, did not have an institution such as the mir, with its village ties and communal ownership of property; accordingly, there was little of a migratory trend. True, as industrialism made headway and trade unions came into being, there arose among some workers an interest in socialism. For Germany was the original home of the two leading socialistic prophets, Karl Marx and Friedrich Engels. Both writers took the land owners and capitalists to task for allegedly exploiting the mass of laborers. Like prophets, they predicted the coming of a social order in which the "exploiters" would be punished and a communal brotherhood of proletarians established. They alone were the spokesmen of a migratory movement in Germany, a movement which, however, was not too widespread and ran counter to the mainstream of German thought.

Exactly, what was this mainstream? It was an outlook which conformed too readily to the expansive rather than interactive pattern. Prominent German writers stood solidly for the old order, or for the martial and heroic spirit so essential to military success; some even asserted that their people were destined to rule the world.

German authors who lived during the period of the Second Reich (1871-1932) differed in their outlook only to an extent from those of the early nineteenth century. Among the latter, Johann Wolfgang von Goethe was, no doubt, the most eminent. Goethe, while having been influenced by the Enlightenment and also international in his perspective, opposed the efforts of German liberals to promote French Revolutionary sentiment in Germany.[28] In fact, he even favored the French Bourbon suppression of the liberal revolt in Spain in 1823.[29] In all his later works, including the masterpiece *Faust*, Goethe sought to reform the individual rather than society, and in this way, too, he appeared to support the aristocratic regime. But being primarily a poet, and not a philosopher, he did not present a system of thought to justify the established order.

For such a presentation we must turn to the writings of Georg Friedrich Hegel, the renowned master of the dialectic and a staunch supporter of the philosophy of statism. Using his famed dialectical approach to history, Hegel attempted to prove that the Prussian state, in his day, was the consummation of human progress. Throughout history, man has progressed in three stages: the Oriental, during which the ruler alone was a free and integrated being; the Classical, when one class similarly fortunate; and now the Germanic, when all citizens are in such happy circumstances. But being free and integrated in this present stage means having the freedom and opportunity to obey those in authority, and, happily, it is Prussia which offers these conditions.

During the succeeding era of the Second Reich, Hegel's greatest disciple in the philosophy of statism was Heinrich von Treitschke. This famous and chauvinistic historian maintained that the state was above and more important than the people comprising it. Indeed, the common rules and morals which are binding on ordinary citizens do not apply to the state. Even a war provoked by the state is not only, at times, justifiable, but desirable, since it strengthens the political organism. In his *Politics,* he contended:

"We learn from history that nothing knits a nation more closely together than war. It makes it worthy of the

28. Peter Eckermann, *Conversations with Goethe,* (Everyman) , 1951, p. 36.
29. *Ibid.,* p. 43.

name of nation as nothing else can, and the extension of existent States is generally achieved by conquest, even if confirmed by treaty, according to the results of the appeal to arms."[30]

Thus, Treitschke would have none of the Chrisian morality or philosophy of Enlightenment which is, at least theoretically, applied to international relations.

From believing in the supremacy of the State over its citizens it is not too great a step to asserting the superiority of one class of people over another. Such a superiority could be realized in the struggle for existence and in the ensuing triumph of the strongest. This was the thesis of Friedrich Wilhelm Nietzsche, the renowned poet-philosopher. The idea that existence is a struggle was advanced earlier by Arthur Schopenhauer, who was one of the first to view the world as a place of discord rather than of harmony. But while Schopenhauer sought escape from this veritable arena, Nietzsche welcomed it as leading to the ascendance of a superrace. To Nietzsche, all forms of religious and political thought which protect the weak and hinder the strong are detrimental, as they prevent such an ascendance; hence, he despised Christianity, democracy, and socialism. The society which he envisioned would be ruled by an elite of vigorous and capable heroes, and in this order of things the common man would be downtrodden. As he stated in his *Will to Power*:

"The belittlement of man must be held as the chief aim for a long while: because what is needed in the first place is a broad basis from which a stronger species of man may arise. To what extent, hitherto, has every stronger species of man arisen but from a substratum of inferior people?"[31]

Nietzsche was almost the lifelong friend of the composer Richard Wagner, since the two men had much in common.

---

30. Treitschke, *Politics*, London: 1916, vol. I, p. 108.
31. Nietzsche, *The Will to Power*, from the *Complete Works*. ed. Oscar Levi, London, 1924, Vol. II, Bk. IV, 890.

Both had been reared in an atmosphere of feudalistic relics and romantic folk lore, in which the deeds of past German heroes were recalled and vividly portrayed. In later life, however, Wagner was more chauvinistic than Nietzsche. In the composer's music dramas and prose writings, the legendary warrior Siegfried comes forth as the leader of the German people. To Wagner, the Germans are destined to rule the world, but in order to demonstrate that they are fated for this role, they must perform acts of valor in the manner of Siegfried.

In effect, it could be said that the theme of German culture, in the late nineteenth century, was the insistence on state supremacy over both the individual from within and the neighboring countries from without. To some writers, this twin purpose could be achieved if proper respect were given to leaders and heroes. To a great extent, the combination of hero-worship and respect for law and order enabled the expansive society of Germany to maintain its full integrity, not only up to but throughout World War I. The crusades of the Teutonic Knights and the sermons of the Lutheran pastors had not been in vain!

The German empire was proclaimed in 1871, the very year in which Italy, too, achieved unification. Moreover, while Germany was unified under the leadership of Prussia, so did Italy become a single state through the efforts of Piedmont-Sardinia. Since Piedmont-Sardinia was, like Prussia, an expansive state, the Italy which emerged was likewise expansive.

It can be said that with respect to her social organization, alone, the new kingdom of Italy was less expansive than Russia or Germany. There was lacking, among the Italians, the influential military aristocracy that one found in the other two countries. Although a nobility, dating from feudal times, did exist, it remained aloof from politics since unification. In fact, the lower chamber of the Italian parliament was generally controlled by a commercial and professional bourgeoisie and a class of landed proprietors who had become wealthy through trade.

But while the nobles were without influence, the royal family and its attendants had power and prestige alike. The king had the authority to convene and dissolve Parliament, he appointed the members of the upper chamber, or senate, and frequently presided over cabinet meetings. In times of crisis, he could assume control of the government and exert virtually dictatorial powers.

Indeed, the king and his court attendants had little regard for parliamentary procedure, or even for civilians! The monarch was almost always surrounded by army officers, and he, himself, rarely appeared in civilian attire.[32] There could be little question as to the pride which the king and court took in their military apparel.

Why was there such military pomp and decorum among the royal entourage? Again, the reason is historical. From medieval times the king's ancestors, the counts of Savoy, had struggled to hold their fief, with its strategic Alpine passes, against several or more rival feudatories. Since the best defense was offense, and the counts were ambitious, besides, they extended their fief, subsequently called Piedmont, until it had become the second largest state in Italy. By the eighteenth century, the counts had become kings, but they still had to reckon with powerful neighbors—France and Austria. However, by recruiting a sizeable army, they fought first on the one side and then on the other, acquiring even more territory, so that by 1850 Piedmont had emerged as the leading Italian principality.

In all these successful ventures the army had played a vital role. Hence, from the advent of unification, it is little wonder that the House of Savoy looked to the military as the answer to the problems of State. In fact, the king and court regarded war as an honorable profession,

---

32. Denis Mack Smith, *Italy: A Modern History*, Ann Arbor, Mich., 1959, p. 29.

and considering the poverty of the country, far too much money was spent on the armed forces.[33] Even long before the era of fascism, the king, the court and a small clique of armament manufacturers steered Italy into stormy international waters; it made little difference to them whether this course of action had parliamentary or popular approval.

On three occasions, during the period from 1871 to 1918, Italy went to war without provocation. The reason was the prompting which the nation received from this small but powerful minority. In 1893, Premier Crispi, sensing that his tenure of office was contingent upon the good will of this clique, embarked on an adventure in east Africa.[34] The result was a disastrous defeat by Ethiopia. A similarly expansionist policy was pursued by Premier Giolitti, in 1912, and for virtually the same reason.[35] This venture was more successful, since Italy was able to acquire Libya. However, the most classic example of the pressure exerted by this influential elite was in 1915, when, against the opposition of Premier Salandra, most of Parliament and the majority of the people, the court negotiated a secret treaty in London, thereby committing Italy to go to war with the Central Powers.[36]

Indeed, though Italy was expansive, the mass of people were less enthusiastic in their support of the ruling hierarchy than was the case in Germany. For in Italy, it was not the spirit of the Reformation, but that of the Renaissance which predominated. This meant that there was far less in the way of self-denial on behalf of the state, and that any respect for authority was tempered by individualism. Then too, owing to the deep-rooted Catholi-

33. *Ibid.*
34. *Ibid.*, pp. 183–84.
35. *Ibid.*, p. 275.
36. *Ibid.*, pp. 296–98.

cism, such respect or devotion was more likely reserved for the pope rather than for a secular ruler.

Since the Italians were spared the German Lutheran teaching that self-denial is a virtue, they were more tolerant of self-gratification. Hence, they were inclined to take life leisurely, although here the climate was an added factor. Their sense of leisure could be seen in the relative disregard of time and the custom of taking the daily siesta. With respect to education, work and recreation, this relaxed pace was the general occasion. A noted example was in their theater-going. A British tourist reported that the reasons the Italians attended the theater were not alone amusement but to find somewhere to spend the long evening hours.[37] This attitude contrasted with the noble but rigid one of the German audience.

Such a relaxation in the expansive pattern was reflected in the cultural life of Italy. Most of the Italian writers only tacitly supported the ruling hierarchy and its policies. While assenting, occasionally, to a declaration of war by their government, they did not look upon military aggression as a virtue in itself; while generally indifferent to humanitarian movements, they did not assert that the masses should be belittled. Rather than rigidly Lutheran, their outlook was that of Catholicism, modified by Humanism.

A blending of Catholic and Humanistic sentiment was to be found in the writings of an earlier but most esteemed of Italian novelists, Alessandro Manzoni. In his famous work, *I Promesi Sposi* (*The Betrothed*), Manzoni draws a distinction between the Catholic clergy who are conservative and those who are progressive and humane. However, Manzoni was hardly a social reformer; rather he believed that through faith alone, and as individuals, can man hope to achieve a better future.

---

37. H. Zimmern, *Italy of the Italians*, London, 1910, p. 141.

More politically conscious than Manzoni was Giuseppe Mazzini, an active leader in the Risorgimento and also a renowned theorist. Just as Manzoni was influenced by Augustine and Thomas Aquinas (c. 1225-1274), so Mazzini was impressed with the ideas held by Dante Alighieri (1265-1321). This most eminent of Italian poets believed in the moral regeneration of man; such was the central theme of his *Divine Comedy*. Mazzini, too, was vitally interested in the moral advancement of humanity; this, he believed, could come about only through a religious and democratic brotherhood of nation-states, having its spiritual center in Rome. With his mystical nationalism and belief in religious brotherhood, Mazzini's thinking bordered on the migratory. However, he alone, among Italian theorists, regarded both the Church and the monarchy as impostors and, significantly, his last years were spent in self-imposed exile.

Mazzini was a definite exception. For the leading Italian authors, of the late nineteenth and early twentieth centuries, either upheld the status quo or were reactionary, although as a group they were not as much so as were their German contemporaries. An outstanding example was the sociologist Vilfredo Pareto, who was somewhat of a cynic. Pareto considered the average man as being fundamentally irrational; only a minority of gifted persons, he thought, are capable of sound reasoning. He doubted, therefore, that a parliamentary government could be effective in steering the ship of state. In its place, he would establish a government by an elite, which is rational and undisturbed by the illogical behavior of a legislature or electorate! Pareto also questioned the value of humanitarian measures. As he stated in his *Mind and Society*:

"Humanitarianism is worthless from the logico-experimental point of view, whether because it has no slightest intrinsic soundness of a scientific character, or more especially because even if, on an assumption devoid of any probability, it had some points of soundness, that fact would not help as regards spurring human beings to the required activities, for human beings are guided primarily by sentiment."[38]

While Pareto stressed the value of logic and experiment to support a conservative domestic policy, the philosopher and historian, Benedetto Croce, justified the Italian imperialism in his day on sentimental grounds. Again, the question of Italy's role in North Africa had arisen. To Croce, the acquisition of territory in this region by Great Britain and France was a kind of humiliation for Italy. This being so, why shouldn't his countrymen have seized Tripoli (Libya) from the Turks, especially since this site of ancient Roman colonies was regarded with sentimental attachment? Such apparent justification of this venture appeared in his *History of Italy*:

"'Italy went to Tripoli, because she could not resign herself to the idea of the French, the English and the Spaniards establishing themselves before her eyes along the African coast, if the Italian flag was not to be planted in any part of it, and if Italy did not share with the rest of Europe in the Europeanization of Africa. She went because she could not accept the setback in which the Abyssinian expedition had involved her in Crispi's time, and because she was no longer what she had been fifteen years before, but was now ready to organize a military expedition and carry it through to victory. She went, in short, for what are known as sentimental reasons: which are, however, as real as any others and, in their own way, as practical."[39]

It is significant that Croce supported the African venture largely because of the virtual proximity of Tripoli to

---

38. Pareto, *The Mind and Society*, New York, 1935, Vol. III, p. 1293.
39. Croce, *A History of Italy*, Oxford, 1929, pp. 259–61.

Italy; he, in contrast to Treitschke and Nietzsche, did not look upon war and imperialism as commendable in themselves.

In fact, of all Italian writers, only Gabriele D'Annunzio, in both word and deed, stood constantly in favor of forceful measures against alleged enemies. This somewhat unbalanced character was famous not only for his verses and short stories, but also for his speeches and political activities, of which the seizure of Fiume, in 1920, was an apt illustration. However, with the chauvinism of D'Annunzio, we are almost in the era of fascism.

All in all, the principal modern Italian writers, Mazzini excepted, were distrustful of the masses, opposed to reform and in favor of territorial expansion. In expressing their ideas, the authors varied considerably as to temperament. Some were optimists, others, pessimists; some were extremely rational in their approach, others, highly emotional. In this variation of temperament they resembled the German writers. Still, the Italians, generally, were not as blatant in their expressions, or extreme in their ideas, as were the Germans.

The milder nature of the Italian literati is to be attributed to the more relaxed atmosphere of the society itself. In Italy, to be sure, the king and court had considerable power. Yet, there was far less in the way of class distinctions, since a Junker-type elite was all but lacking. Furthermore, the Spartan-like education, very strict attendance to duty and regimen of self-discipline, so common in Germany, and particularly in Prussia, were not apparent in Italy. In short, Italian society, while expansive, was not rigidly so, as far as the individual was concerned.

Journeying from Italy to another and distant country, Great Britain, we come to a society which is quite opposite: Interactive, rather than expansive, and yet far more self-denying than self-gratifying. The interactive character of British society could be seen in its socio-political organization; the self-denial, in its Puritan way of life. Both traits profoundly influenced British culture.

The socio-political organization, indeed, the power structure of Britain, in the late nineteenth century, was hardly that of an expansive society. There was a sovereign who reigned but didn't rule, and whose court was a center of bourgeois more than of aristocratic convention. There was an aristocracy, not so much of birth as of wealth, with new members continually being admitted to its ranks. There was an established Church, but complete religious freedom.

The British monarch had little of the prerogative that was enjoyed by the king of Italy, or even by the emperor of Germany. True, the king of England had the authority to convene and dissolve Parliament, and he was consulted on major issues. But he was expected to confer with parliamentary leaders before making a move.

The British peerage, like nobles elsewhere, had its land and titles. But by Continental standards, it was an upstart nobility. Actually, the medieval nobles, in England, had all but disappeared with the War of the Roses (1453-1485). The struggle between York and Lancaster was also the final struggle of the feudal lords to assert their declining leadership, but with the victory of the Lancastrian Tudors, what was left of the feudality retreated into the background. During the period of absolute monarchy which followed, country gentlemen who were rich and had faithfully served the king were admitted to the rank of peer; wealthy merchants and stock company shareholders purchased estates and became squires, on which occasion some obtained responsible positions in local government.

From the Tudor period (1485-1603) to the Victorian Age (1837-1901), this process of ascendance on the social ladder continued. Ascendance depended more upon ownership of wealth and meritorious service, whether in government, science or war, than upon geneology. In all likelihood, monetary and landed possession was the principal determinant of status, a characteristic of British society that was observed by the French historian Alexis de Tocqueville, on a journey to Britain in 1837.[40] On the other hand, the fact that the British nobility had the blood of commoners in its veins was known throughout the Continent. Indeed, it is said that in the decades following World War I, the aristocratic envoys from Great Britain were regarded with contempt by the peers of the former Austrian empire.[41] But this only proves that British society did not have the rigid class distinctions so characteristic of central Europe.

In contrast to the Austrian and German chancellors, the British prime ministers were from all classes. Through the late nineteenth and early twentieth centuries, only the Marquis of Salisbury, the Earl of Rosebury and Sir Arthur Balfour belonged to the nobility. On the contrary, William Gladstone, Benjamin Disraeli, Henry Campbell-Bannerman and Herbert Asquith were the sons of prominent manufacturers.[42] In fact, David Lloyd George, a leader in the "radical" faction of the Liberal party, came from the lower middle class.

The interactive pattern could be observed not only in the background of important political personalities. It was also to be seen in the attitude of the average British citizen toward government officials. Whereas the Germans were subservient toward even the lowest public servant, due to their respect for the uniform, the British were not so impressed by persons in semimilitary attire. Accordingly, the Britons regarded all government officials, regardless of rank, as being no better than themselves.

---

40. Tocqueville, *Journeys to England and Ireland*, New Haven, 1958, pp. 90–91.
41. R. Bruce Lockart, *Retreat from Glory*, London, 1934, p. 59.
42. F. Gosses, *The Management of British Foreign Policy before the First World War*, Leiden, 1948, p. 23.

Equally indicative of the interactive pattern was the very framework of government. The British parliament comprised lords as well as commoners, but it was the House of Commons, more than the House of Lords, that was the heart of the political organism. This was particularly true after the passage of the Parliament Act, in 1911. This lower but powerful body represented all classes, though the representation from the industrialists, traders and squires was most influential. In the affairs of state, the prime minister and cabinet, all responsible to parliament, made the decisions, which, in turn, were subject to parliamentary approval. An unpopular move by the prime minister would result in an exhaustive interrogation by angry members, especially if the latter had public support. Furthermore, on vital questions, such as the declaration of war, ratification of peace treaties and drawing up of international agreements, a vote by Parliament was necessary.

While Parliament was the political center of the nation, the court was its social nucleus. The king, or queen, and royal retinue set the pace for manners and customs. But then the code of etiquette upheld in the court reflected the temper and mood of the country. Since the national mood and temper were predominantly those of a middle class, as befitting an interactive society, so were the morals upheld in the palace. Here, there was little of the army-like atmosphere that one found in the Italian court. Moreover, there was relatively less regard for military glory and greater respect for business enterprise. Prominent merchants and industrialists were honored by the British court as much as were generals or admirals. The palace was, indeed, a standard-bearer for Roundhead, as contrasted with Cavalier, convention. A notable example was the abolition of dueling, in both military and civilian life, during the reign of Queen Victoria and Prince Albert.[43]

---

43. W. Debelius, *England*, London, 1923, p. 230.

This ban was in decided contrast to the high regard for fencing which was held in imperial Germany.

On the other hand, the court also reflected the strict morals maintained with respect to sex and marriage. Here, Britain resembled rather than differed from Germany. Sexual promiscuity and extramarital relations were severely censored. Then too, with the progress of the Victorian Age, the Puritan morals, so characteristic of the middle class, found their way into the upper and lower social strata, and they influenced life in its many phases, recreation as well as work. It could be said that one reason for the popularity of team sports, both in the schools and beyond the campus, was their role in providing outlets for young men. With teams combatting for the final victory, the players, and even the spectators, would be too exhausted to have affairs. Such self-denial of pleasure was practiced in Germany as well as in Britain. But whereas in Germany students at Jena, Halle, Leipzig, and Bonn took vows to remain chaste,[44] as well as engaged in gymnastics, those at Oxford and Cambridge had their interest in sex diverted by fierce competition in the sports arena. The strenuous team sports, together with the custom of fagging adhered to in the British middle schools, also attested to the self-denying character of society in the island kingdom.

As British society was, at once, interactive and self-denying, numerous writers, in the Victorian Age, expressed sympathy for the poor and, yet, were distrustful of the majority. Many favored reforms, but only to the extent that they would not interfere with the right of the fortunate few to make their way in the world. On the question of war and peace, most authors were pacifists, but some expressed belligerence if Britain were merely insulted. This belligerent attitude arose from the somewhat stifling character of Puritan society itself, but still the writers did not seek glory in war or conquest.

---

44. H. A. Taine, *Notes on England*, The Hague, 1957, p. 96.

In an earlier chapter, I spoke of Samuel Johnson as exemplifying English thought in the eighteenth century. For the Victorian Age, Charles Dickens would be among those highly representative. That Dickens was, to a degree, humane in his attitude toward the poor is evident in *Oliver Twist, David Copperfield, A Christmas Carol,* and other works. Even in *A Tale of Two Cities* he portrayed the misery of the French artisans and laborers who lived under the Ancien Regime. True, like Goethe, he was shocked at the excesses of the French Revolution, without fully appreciating its achievements. Still, Goethe was interested primarily in individual improvement under the status quo and expressed little concern for social conditions. Dickens, on the contrary, would try to remedy these conditions, though he would do so by urging the wealthy to be charitable rather than by pressing for social legislation. In other respects, Dickens was actually conservative. His dislike of the French Jacobins was due, in large measure, to his English upbringing; and in his portrayal of family life, and particularly of women, he held steadfast to Puritan ethics.

Sharing Dickens's humantarianism, and also national and Puritan sentiments, was Lord Macaulay, historian and Whig politician. Macaulay was a staunch defender of British parliamentarianism and free trade. Moreover, his attitude toward the common people, whether British or foreign, was generally humane; for him the thought that they should be belittled was out of the question. At the same time, owing quite possibly to a rigid discipline in a church school when young, Macaulay had enough of the fighter in him to assert that Britain was justified in going to war with China. This opinion he expressed in the following excerpt from a speech delivered in the House of Commons, in 1840:

"He [the Emperor of China] had a perfect right to keep out opium and to keep out silver, if he could do so by means consistent with morality and public law. If his officers seized a chest of the forbidden drug, we were not entitled to complain, nor did we complain. But when, finding that they could not suppress the contraband trade by just means, they resorted to means flagrantly unjust, when they imprisoned our innocent countrymen, when they insulted our sovereign in the person of her representative, then it became our duty to demand satisfaction."[45]

Still, Macaulay, unlike Treitschke, did not look upon war as a means of strengthening the State; nor did he justify conquest on the basis of sentiment, as did Croce. Instead, like a true Puritan, he defended punitive action, or even imperialism, on moral grounds.

Classical liberalism, Puritanism and national pride received a further boost in the verses of Alfred Lord Tennyson, British poet laureate. Tennyson wrote enthusiastically of British heroism, both on the field of battle and in the industrial workshop; he also stood in favor of free trade as heralding a long era of peace. But Victorian morality could be seen in his account of King Arthur and of other legendary characters.

In fact, a veritable hero-worship had already come to the fore in British literature, and the basis of this tendency was Puritanism itself, with its distinction between the "elect" and the "mob." Early in the century, Lord Byron, a true idealist, had set a precedent for heroism in both verse and deed. But it was Thomas Carlyle who became its standard-bearer. Himself a Calvinist, Carlyle considered historical movements to be the work of "great men." Indeed, he was so concerned with the progress and well-being of the elect that he doubted the merits of social reform, although in contrast to Nietzsche, he did show sympathy for the poor. Carlyle's hero-worship and the prominent place which he held in British literary circles

---

45. Macaulay, *Speeches on Politics & Literature* (Everyman) , 1917, p. 172.

were an indication that Britain, while interactive, was not completely so.

A humane outlook, mingled with a distrust of the general public, appeared even in the writings of John Stuart Mill, an eminent reformer. Mill strongly advocated such social security measures as sickness, accident and old-age insurance, as well as land redistribution. But he was wary of the masses, and felt that since people acted in self-interest, they could not be trusted to vote wisely. The tyranny which he feared was the tyranny of the majority, and he would protect the individual against it, even if it meant restricting the ballot. For Mill was worried that a creative minority would be stifled by the mediocrity of the general public. However, while voicing opposition to a democratic form of government, he also opposed the forcible seizure of power by an elite:

"No government by a democracy or a numerous aristocracy, either in its political acts or in the opinions, qualities and tone of mind which it fosters, ever did or could rise above mediocrity, except in so far as the sovereign Many have let themselves be guided . . . by the counsels and influence of a more highly gifted and instructed One or Few. The initiation of all wise and noble things comes and must come from individuals; generally at first from some one individual. The honour and glory of the average man is that he is capable of following that initiative; that he can be led to wise and noble things, and be led to them with his eyes open. I am not countenancing the sort of hero-worship which applauds the strong man of genius for forcibly seizing on the government of the world and making it do his bidding in spite of itself. All he can claim is freedom to point out the way. The power of compelling others into it is not only inconsistent with the freedom and development of all the rest, but corrupting to the strong man himself."[46]

46. Mill, "On Liberty," in *Utilitarianism, Liberty and Representative Government* (Everyman), 1944, Chap. III.

Although he distrusted the masses, Mill's sharp difference with Pareto over the desirability of political power seizure is significant.

Less sympathetic with the common man and more of a rugged individualist was Herbert Spencer, the son of a Methodist minister. Spencer was a firm believer in the Darwinian theory of natural selection. In fact, so convinced was he that evolution should take its course that he opposed all legislation which protected the "incompetent" and thus prevented the more capable individuals from succeeeding. This laissez-faire attitude was quite consistent with his pet phrase, "survival of the fittest."

It could be argued that by believing in the survival of the fittest, Spencer resembled Nietzsche. But the analogy would be incorrect. Nietzsche would do everything possible to degrade the mass of humanity; Spencer would do nothing. Nietzsche regarded war as the means by which a superman would emerge; Spencer cared neither for war nor for supermen and hoped that in the future a world federation would arise to promote peace. It was on this question, especially, that the British evolutionist showed a more humane attitude.

Thus, British literature, too, reflected the trend of society. There was, in general, sympathy for those who were victimized by enclosure and industrialization. Yet, more often than not, humane considerations were mingled with a wariness toward the public. On another question, that of peace and war, there was division of opinion, a few authors favoring war, and even expansion, on behalf of moral principles. For owing to the Puritan background and way of life, British society had not completely abandoned its expansive heritage. Yet, if British authorship were to be compared to Italian, and especially to German, of the same period, it would show a considerably more humane and pacifistic trend.

Great Britain was not alone in being a major interactive

European society; France, too, shared this honor. Furthermore, while the British were generally a self-denying people, the French were more tolerant of self-gratification, a characteristic which, in turn, enabled them to be even more interactive than the islanders to the north. For, as we noted earlier, the freedom from Puritanism and from the concern with one's economic status had allowed the French to surpass the British in the extent of their revolution.

It was the upheaval of 1789 which marked the beginning of republicanism and of bourgeois supremacy in France. Yet, the victory of the bourgeoisie was by no means assured. From the advent of the Restoration, in 1815, to the establishment of the Third Republic, in 1875, the ultraconservative members of the aristocracy and clergy were constantly working behind the scenes to undo the work of the Revolution. Indeed, even the wealthier among the bourgeoisie were at times willing to abandon the principles of the Revolution, as long as their interests were safeguarded by the regime. And, as often as not, the regime, in turn, appeared to be serving only a small minority. The restored Bourbon monarchy, and Charles X (r. 1824-1830) in particular, catered to the peers and bishops; the ministry of Louis Philippe (r. 1830-1848) favored the wealthier of the merchants, industrialists, and bankers. Hence, on two occasions, in 1830 and in 1848, after the artisans had taken to the barricades in protest, the petit bourgeoisie and their peasant allies also reminded the reactionaries, though less violently, that the Revolution was in France to stay.

The February upheaval of 1848 saw the proclamation of the Second French Republic under Louis Napoleon Bonaparte; this regime was subsequently transformed into the Second Empire (1853-1871). Admittedly, the Second Empire was a kind of autocracy. Still, in order to keep his throne, Louis Napoleon had to pursue policies which were readily acceptable to the bourgeoisie. In fact, even the disastrous war of 1870 was, in part, due to French middle class hatred of Prussian conservatism and fear for national security.

With the defeat at Sedan, the Bonapartist regime was discredited, and the Third Republic, which followed, was, no doubt, more democratic. Whereas the Second Empire had relied upon the tacit support of the numerous property holders—petit entrepreneurs, shopkeepers, peasant proprietors and artisans, the Third Republic, with its parliamentary system, depended on their active vote. It was this huge middle class which was the prop of the republic.

Here, a comparison can be made between France and Britain. There is little question that in Britain the parliamentary system was older and that it rested on a firmer foundation. But, then too, the British system depended on a ruling aristocracy, an aristocracy of wealth to be sure, yet, a set governing class. In France, on the contrary, class distinctions, even in the mid-nineteenth century, were not as apparent as in Britain or elsewhere. Economic differences between rich and poor in France were far less obvious. Moreover, during the era of the Third Republic, persons even in high positions boasted of their humble origin.[47] Two presidents—Fallières and Loubet—were of peasant or working-class origin, and Faure, while the son of a petty merchant, learned his trade as a tanner by serving as a workingman and apprentice.[48]

Alongside the interactive aspects of French society, there were its self-gratifying characteristics. This is not to say that self-denial was nonexistent in France. Such was far from the case, when considering the heavy assignments required of students in all levels of education and the thrifty habits of the French peasant. But the French were

47. E. H. Barker, *France of the French,* London, 1908, pp. 31–32.
48. *Ibid.*

not as obsessed with the urge to be "successful" as were the British, and they were not as inhibited in their self-expression. This greater freedom was due to their never having revolted against the Church and, therefore, not feeling the necessity of providing moral grounds for having done so. Among the French, it was not the spirit of the Reformation, but rather that of the Renaissance and Enlightenment which was prevalent.

For one thing, the French were more candid than the British and Germans in matters of sex. I am not implying that the French were promiscuous; this would be far from the truth. But the value system among them differed from that of, particularly, the Anglo-Saxons. An American visitor to France in the 1880's observed that as long as a Frenchman was a good father and husband and provided well for his family, he would be pardoned for having an affair out of wedlock now and then.[49] This attitude contrasted with the English-American, which demanded complete loyalty on the part of the husband and regarded ill-temper at home, or failure to provide, as being of secondary importance.

The greater sexual freedom in France caused a student's life to be less rigorous physically than in the Protestant countries. In the French schools, one could hardly find the rigid body training and dueling, that he saw in Germany, or the fagging and emphasis on team sports, so common in Britain. There was discipline, to be sure, but it was a mental discipline, requiring the student to spend many hours in study. This requirement was directly related to the age-long Church and state controversy over control of French education. From medieval times, the clergy had stressed learning and erudition. Therefore, by demanding much from the students in the way of intellectual achievement, the Republic could justify its ouster

---

49. B. Wendell, *The France of Today*, New York, 1907, pp. 140–41.

of the Church, in 1905, as the organization to supervise public instruction.

For another, British and American travellers noted the intellectual honesty prevailing in France.[50] This contrasted with the reticence in Britain, where people of the middle class were reluctant to express unpopular opinions. Foreigners who frequented the Paris cafes and were present at the salons were impressed with the extent to which the French surpassed others in the art of candid conversation.

In a country where the salon abounded and topics of the day were freely discussed, it would naturally follow that such candor would be reflected in the literary life. Hence it is not suprising that three leading French novelists of the first half of the century—Stendhal (Henri Beyle), Honoré de Balzac, and Victor Hugo—took a lively interest in politics. Stendhal, the first psychological novelist and a staunch supporter of the Revolution, portrayed, in *The Red and the Black,* the helplessness of his hero, Julien Sorel, amid what he regarded as a society controlled by the royalty and clergy. Balzac, who wrote later, was a foe, not of Charles X, but of Louis Philippe, and he took the bourgeoisie to task for their pettiness and parsimony. Hugo was the arch-enemy of Louis Napoleon and his semi-dictatorial methods. Like Dickens, he sympathized with the poor and unfortunate. But whereas Dickens proposed Christian charity and emigration to the colonies as the solution to poverty, Hugo stood for social legislation at home.

This brings us to a difference between the French and British reformers. The British authors favored reform, but being Puritans, they were also anxious to preserve the independence of the individual in the face of social legislation. Among the principal French writers in the nineteenth century, only the political theorist, Alexis de

---

50. H. Lynch, *French Life in Town and Country,* London, 1901, p. 65.

Tocqueville, a Norman nobleman, shared with the British a desire for reform coupled with a warning over the tyranny of the majority. But most of the French intellectuals were free from either an aristocratic or Puritan atmosphere and, therefore, could be more consistent. They not only thought that the condition of the less fortunate should be improved; they also proposed social systems by which such improvement could be realized.

The systems which most French writers envisioned were within the framework of a capitalistic economy. In this way they differed from their predecessor, Rousseau, who had advocated doing away with private property. But Rousseau's desire to return to a "state of Nature" was due to his having lived in an expansive society from which he felt alienated. The nineteenth-century authors, on the contrary, were members of a society which, despite recurrent political reaction, had become interactive.

An early writer who believed that there should be reforms, but within the established economic framework, was Count Henri de Saint-Simon. Erroneously, Saint-Simon has been referred to as a socialist. Actually, he would preserve private property, while having society devote its principal efforts on behalf of the common man. Saint-Simon would have the government directed by experts—scientists, capitalists and literati—who would be proficient in the task of administration; his mills and factories would be cooperative enterprises of engineers, capitalists and laborers.

The most renowned student of Saint-Simon was Auguste Comte, the founder of sociology. Comte proposed a system whereby a group of specialists, trained in the science of fact-finding, would govern. His administration would pursue a policy of enlightened reform. Here, Comte differed decidedly from Spencer, the leading British sociologist. Rather, he resembled Mill in being a staunch advocate of social security measures and of sex equality;

in fact, it was from Comte that Mill obtained his progressive ideas on these subjects. But whereas Mill distrusted the opinion of the majority, Comte welcomed it, considering it to be a moral force in society. For while Mill was anxious to preserve the right (and this could mean the privilege) of the individual, Comte would protect society from what could be selfish interests. As he stated in his "Positive Polity":

"It is the first of duties to concentrate all the efforts of society upon the common good. And in this there is a more direct reference to the working class than to any other; first, on account of their immense numerical superiority, and, secondly, because the difficulties by which their life is surrounded require special interference to a degree which for other classes would be unnecessary. From this point of view is it a principle which all true republicans may accept. It is, in fact, identical with what we have laid down as the universal basis of morality, the direct and permanent preponderance of social feeling over all personal interests."[51]

British and French writers differed, to a degree, not only with respect to social reform, but also in their attitude toward war. Whereas some of the British were ready to wage war for moral purposes, the French were almost invariably pacifists. Saint-Simon maintained that wars were caused by the inability of the workers to purchase what they produced, a situation which leads to overproduction and a struggle for markets. Comte conceived of history as human development in three stages: the first, or primitive, was the warlike; the last, or industrial, the scientific and peaceful stage. De Tocqueville, too, considered peace to be a mark of progress and civilization.

Jules Michelet, perhaps the most nationalistic of French historians, was less inclined than Lord Macaulay to find even a moral justification for aggression. In a work on

---

51. Comte, *System of Positive Polity*, London, 1875, Vol. I, p. 108.

the French Revolution, Michelet referred to the pacificism of those who participated in this dynamic upsurge:

"Her [France's] heroes, her invincible heroes, were the most pacific of human beings. Hoche, Marceau, Desaix and Kleber are deplored by friends and foes as the champions of peace; they are mourned by the Nile and by the Rhine, nay by war itself—by the inflexible Vendee.

"France had so completely identified herself with this thought that she did her utmost to restrain herself from achieving conquests. Every nation needing the same blessing—liberty—and pursuing the same right, whence could war possibly arise? Could the Revolution, which, in its principles, was but the triumph of right, the resurrection of justice, the tardy reaction of thought against brute force—could it, without provocation, have recourse to violence?"[52]

The interest in social reform and in the prevention of war was of no less concern to the realistic French novelists who wrote in the latter half of the century. Among them, two—Emile Zola and Anatole France (Jacques Thibault) —were outstanding in their presentation of these themes. Zola, the founder of naturalism, submitted numerous volumes, in which he depicted certain difficult conditions among the working class; for example, in *Germinal,* he described the hardships of the miners. Also in *The Attack on the Mill* and other stories, he showed the irony of war. Equally influential was Anatole France who in his day was the leading personality in the French literary world. In such masterpieces as *Penguin Island* and *Revolt of the Angels,* he poured scorn upon the lack of understanding in human society and all too frequent recourse to violence. Anatole France was often accused of being cynical; however, one could also sense that he really desired to see established a harmonious social order that allowed for

---

52. Michelet, *A Historical View of the French Revolution,* trans. C. Cocks, London, 1912, pp. 3-4.

security as well as freedom. It is significant that in later life both Zola and Anatole France belonged to the Radical Republican party, which, in the 1890's, helped to introduce legislation to assist workers and was urging ministries to pursue pacifistic foreign policies.

Generally, it could be said that in France there was as much sentiment for reform as there was in Britain, and without the dire concern with individual privilege that one found in the island kingdom. In being free from this concern, the French authors could propose systems or support measures which would do more to curtail personal privilege and a trend toward economic monopoly. Also, there was, among them, even less enthusiasm for imperialism and empire-building.

The comparatively mild attitude of the French intellectuals arose from the truly interactive nature of their society and from the greater allowance of self-gratification. In France, more than in the four other major European societies, did politics function upon a broad basis and were class lines thinly drawn; in France, more than elsewhere, was there freedom of expression.

On the other end of the scale were Germany and Russia. To be sure, the social stratification and concentration of power were even greater in Russia than in Germany. However, owing to their historical and religious setting, the Germans were far more inclined to uphold the established order; also, they were decidedly more restrained in their speech and behavior than were the Russians. Accordingly, the German intellectuals, in contrast to the Russian, displayed a feeling of aggression toward other states and a contempt for the common people that were quite in keeping with the needs of an expansive society.

In between the two extremes were the Italians and British. Like the French, a comparatively self-gratifying people, the Italians were more leisurely and less inclined to conform to a set pattern of behavior than were the

Northerners. But then, the interactive British, in turn, were free from government by intrigue, and at the hands of a narrow court circle. Still, class lines, particularly economic, did exist in Britain, although an individual with sufficient opportunity and initiative could surmount them. However, since most Britons could not scale the economic and social ladder, many, at least, emigrated and became successful colonizers.

E. The Interactive Society of the United States: A Scene of Likeness and Discrepancy

Crossing the Atlantic near the close of the eighteenth century, we would see a flourishing society on the other side. For in 1790, land that had been formerly British colonies and was now the United States was the scene of growing economic activity. In the new American republic there were many bustling coastal settlements and several thriving cities, each having their shipyards, fishing fleets, warehouses, workshops, and carriage depots. Away from the towns, and particularly along the river valleys, there was rolling farm and grazing land, where individual farmers were busily at work, harvesting grain or tending livestock. Beyond the tilled acres, there were seemingly endless regions of virgin land and timber. Indeed, the United States, more than any contemporary society, gave promise of a bright future.

With respect not only to the economic, but also to the socio-political character of the new nation, there was reason to believe that here an ideal interactive society was emerging. Due in part to the absence of a feudal tradition, there was hardly a manorial system. To be sure, there were large landholdings in the middle states, near the Eastern seaboard. But during the American Revolution, many extensive properties, formerly owned by loyal-

ists, were confiscated and sold in smaller lots to patriot
farmers. Most of the wealthy loyalists had lived in the
middle states, while the planters in the South had supported the patriot cause. Accordingly, by 1790, it was
mainly in the South, and along the coast, that one could
see large holdings; elsewhere, farming was carried on principally by small independent proprietors. There was little
left of what was to be a pretentious aristocracy. In the
towns and few cities, too, it was the small enterprise which
predominated. The shipyards, warehouses and workshops
were owned and managed by persons who were on friendly
terms with their employees. Class distinctions were not
too much in evidence.

Moreover, the political system tended in the direction
of republicanism. The election of a president and con-
gress, though by indirect means, marked the beginning.
Admittedly, in South Carolina, Virginia, Maryland, New
York, and Massachusetts, there were property qualifica-
tions for voting and holding office; here, public affairs
were directed by wealthy squires, merchants and shipowners. But in the other states, the majority of small farmers, backwoodsmen, and mechanics were obtaining the
franchise.

The trend toward comparative equality continued well
into the nineteenth century. This century commenced
with the Jeffersonian era (1801-1808), and Thomas
Jefferson, himself, was an enemy to all aristocratic privilege and pretension. Jefferson's dislike of class distinctions was due in large measure to his having been born
and raised in the rugged Piedmont country in Virginia,
a section of the state that contrasted with the more aristocratic Tidewater districts. But he was also influenced
by the people he met when having served as minister to
France. In Paris, Jefferson became a close friend of the
philosopher Condorcet, in whose home he also conversed
with the latter's cultured wife, the French Revolutionary

leader Abbé Sièyes, and the physiocrat Turgot.[53] With these exponents of Enlightened opinion, Jefferson exchanged ideas and found that he shared their views. Like Condorcet, he was a republican; like the Abbé Sieyès, he believed that there is only one estate in society, and not three; like Turgot, he thought that the most contented society is one consisting of small farmers and shopkeepers.

Upon his return to America, Jefferson encouraged his countrymen to abolish the English land laws of primogeniture and entail, and they readily agreed. With the victory of the Jeffersonian Republicans in the presidential election in 1800, these land laws became a thing of the past. Also swept aside, at least temporarily, was the political monopoly of the leading bankers, shipowners and merchants who had exerted influence through the Federalist party.

The process underway in the Jeffersonian era was accelerated in the Jacksonian (1829-1837), when virtually all citizens had secured the franchise. Andrew Jackson, a frontiersman, disliked the still highly influential bankers along the seaboard and the experienced but condescending class of government officials. Accordingly, he refused to renew the charter for the United States Bank. He also introduced the spoils system, whereby any man, regardless of birth but with sufficient integrity, could qualify for public office.

From the Jacksonian era to the outbreak of the Civil War, the forces which stood for equal rights marched steadily forward. During the administration of Abraham Lincoln they could claim two more victories: the Homestead Act and the Emancipation Proclamation. By 1863, it seemed as though the dream of Jefferson, and, we may add, of Benjamin Franklin, Patrick Henry, and Thomas Paine—of a republic of small proprietors, all sharing in

---

53. Phillips Russell, *Jefferson, Champion of the Free Mind*, New York, 1956, pp. 95–96.

political participation—was becoming a reality. Indeed, following the surrender at Appomattox and the elimination of the Southern slave owners, there was ample ground for believing in the essential nobility of man.

However, it is one of the ironies of history that American westward expansion, which, at first, helped to promote the trend toward equality of opportunity, was to bring about the reverse tendency. For in the decades following the defeat of the South, the scene changed. It was now the era of huge land concessions to railroads. While railroad building was certainly an asset to national development, it was accompanied by gross abuse. Many homesteaders were, through underhanded means, deprived of their property, and those that remained and wished to sell their produce in Eastern markets were victimized by high freight rates. Hence, the West and the South were seeing the rise of a debt-ridden farmer.

Not much later, it was the epoch of the trusts, those huge industrial combines, which, by their very magnitude, were capable of stifling individual initiative. Though also a boon to economic advancement, their ascendance was likewise marked by social problems. Having ample resources and a large labor force at their disposal, the trusts were able to undersell the small enterpriser and come near to monopolizing industry. Many who worked in these gigantic firms suffered from the impersonality of the organization and loss of independence, as well as from an inability to put money aside. For the American worker, more than for the immigrant European, an inability to save and a keen sense of dependence were hard to bear, because he had been taught to become a "self-made man." But how could he become self-made when he had so little chance of putting money aside to establish a small business? Even if he were so fortunate, would he not suffer from the competition of the larger concerns? And, finally, would he not, like millions of others, be the victim of over-speculation and business crises, which all too frequently plagued the American scene. There is little doubt that he would.

The feeling that one should be self-made and "successful" was Puritan-inspired. For all good Calvinists believed that if one were successful, he would be a member of the "elite." While, in the nineteenth century, this idea was losing strength, the urge to be a success had become a deeply ingrained habit.

That Puritanism was interwoven into the social fabric there could be little doubt. Over the daily habits and morals of the people its presence could be felt. The Americans, like their British cousins, were very reluctant to tolerate any breach of the established family and sexual norms. This applied not only to behavior, but even to conversations on these topics. In fact, in the average small town community, conversation on any topic was generally standardized, though less so than in England. Americans, too, sought diversion in team sports, and if this were not sufficient, there was plenty that could be done on the farm or in the tool shop. For idleness was the cardinal sin.

The only communities where there was some originality of opinion, at least on the subjects of religion and philosophy, was along the eastern seaboard, and in those centers where the Enlightenment had secured a foothold. It was here that early disagreement with the Calvinistic theology appeared. At first, the religious revolt was expressed by an adherence to Deism; later, it emerged as Unitarianism and, finally, as Transcendentalism. While the Puritans stressed the depravity or, at least, the ineptitude of man (a minority of mankind being the exception), the Unitarians and Transcendentalists spoke of his essential worth.

The reference to Transcendentalism brings us to the subject of literature. In the fertile field of American authorship we can see a diversion into two principal schools:

the one Transcendentalist; the other Puritan. Significantly, during the early and middle decades of the nineteenth century, when a near equalitarianism was making inroads, the Transcendental literature, a literature also of reform, was by far the most popular. Later, reformism, though still vigorous, is threatened by a literature of disillusion, a kind of neo-Calvinism, in which man is portrayed as being depraved and, therefore, of little value in the scheme of things.

It was natural that a movement against any form of oppression, such as slavery, would be preceded by an anti-Puritan rebellion. A pioneer in this rebellion was William Ellery Channing. An enthusiastic reader of the French philosophers, and particularly of Rousseau, Channing was in the vanguard of the movement for a more humane religion. In his sermons, he spoke of the love rather than of the severity of God and maintained that man is basically good instead of evil. Channing's call for a milder theology was answered by two other distinguished preachers: Theodore Parker and Margaret Fuller. Both Parker and Fuller joined Channing in becoming Unitarians; both contended that the core of any true religion is not salvation for oneself, but concern for the present welfare of society.

The new approach to religion gained in momentum when, in 1836, Ralph Waldo Emerson, a Unitarian minister, wrote *On Nature,* in which he stated that every man has within him freedom, creativity, and divinity. As such, he can certainly attain to a democratic and harmonious society. It is significant that Emerson was profoundly stirred by the political and social issues of his day.

Indeed, with the nobility of man established in the literary world, men of letters eagerly took part in reform. William Cullen Bryant stood for free trade, free soil, and free men; John Greenleaf Whittier was also ardent in his denunciation of the South's "peculiar institution"; so, too, was Henry David Thoreau, transcendentalist and physiocrat, who was a staunch supporter of the small farmer in his attempt to secure land at a low price. Together, Emerson, Bryant, Whittier, and Thoreau looked hopefully to the fulfillment of the Jeffersonian dream; together, they saw in its realization the unfolding of the rational and divine in man.

Transcendentalism, with its belief in the nobility of man, was given almost final literary expression by Walt Whitman. In *Leaves of Grass,* Whitman conceived of a vast "similitude" among all things and which showed the handiwork of a kindly Oversoul. Even in the wake of Appomattox, when he showed disappointment over the postwar scene, Whitman continued to believe in the inherent ability and worth of man. In the following passage, he contended that it is the duty of any government to evoke these commendable traits:

"We believe the ulterior project of political and all other government, (having, of course, provided for the police, the safety of life, property, and for the basic statute and common law, and their administration, always first in order) to be among the rest, not merely to rule, to repress disorder, etc., but to develop, to open up to cultivation, to encourage the possibilities of all beneficent and manly outcroppage, and of that inspiration for independence, and the pride and self-respect latent in all characters."[54]

Thus, while at times unhappy with the current American scene, Whitman was never pessimistic with respect to man's potentialities and inherent nature.

For an example of pessimism, we must turn to the works of a later literary giant, Mark Twain (Samuel Clemens). In his early career, he believed in the nobility of man, but it was a nobility, he thought, that was in danger of being corrupted by industrial civilization. His heroes—

---

54. Whitman, "Democratic Vistas," from *Complete Poetry, Selected Prose and Letters,* ed. E. Holloway, London, 1938, p. 675.

Huckleberry Finn and Jim—are pure and virtuous in contrast to their urbane environment with its hypocrisy. In later life, and due to his disgust at the corruption and monopoly, which were emerging, as well as to personal sorrow, Twain, who was of Puritan origin, succumbed to Calvinistic concepts. In his last works and public utterances, he scorned the "stupidity" of mankind.

Mark Twain's career marked a transition from optimism to pessimism in American literature. True, there did follow the era of those reformers known as "muckrakers," who portrayed social evils with the expectation that they would be remedied. Yet, the dominant theme in the novels of Theodore Dreiser and Jack London was humanity's inherent lust and brutality.

In 1916, Edwin A. Robinson composed his poetic masterpiece, *The Man Against the Sky*. In this veritable epic, the author portrayed the futility of those idealists who try to swim against the tide of circumstances. For Robinson saw a society, or even a world, victimized by materialization and human depravity. In the following verse, Robinson has such a dreamer say pathetically:

> Now lead me to the newest of hotels, . . .
> And let your spleen be undeceived:
> This ruin is not myself, but someone else:
> I haven't failed: I've merely not achieved.[55]

The Man Against the Sky appeared just prior to the American entry into World War I. The aftermath of this involvement, together with the hard times which followed, only intensified the disillusion. For the nation had embarked on a crusade to "save the world for democracy," but, as with many crusades, the dreams which inspired them were shattered on the rocks of reality.

If the people had been militarists, and had gone to war

---

55. Robinson, "Old Trails," from *The Man Against the Sky*, in *Collected Poems*, New York, 1954.

for the love of conquest, it would not have led to such feelings of dejection. But, fortunately, the United States has been interactive, rather than expansive, and her citizens more inclined to pacificism. Significantly, almost every renowned American intellectual from Jefferson and Emerson to William James and John Dewey has been opposed to imperialism. Even George Bancroft, one of America's most nationalistic historians, said the following regarding the seizure of Indian lands by Anglo-Saxons:

"Feeble as they were, their [the English] presence alarmed the red man; for it implied the design to occupy the country, which for ages had been his own. His canoe could no longer quiver on the bosom of the St. Mary's, or pass into the clear waters of the Ohio, without passing by the British flag. By what right was that banner unfurled in the west? What claim to the red man's forest could the English derive from victories over the French? The latter seemed no more to be masters but rather companions and friends. Enemies now appeared, arrogant in their pretensions, insolent toward those whom they superceded, driving away their Catholic priests, and introducing the traffic in rum which till then had been effectually prohibited. Since the French must go, no other nation should take their place. The red men must vindicate their right to their own heritage."[56]

In summary, it could be said that American thought, like American society, showed the combined, though frequently opposing, influence of Great Britain and France. From Great Britain, more than from France, came the solid and durable political structure and, at the same time, the scorn for idleness, or even for leisure. From Britain, also, came the strict family and sexual mores and zest for team sports. From France, more than from Britain, came the belief in the worth of man, the zeal for reform

---

56. Bancroft, *History of the United States of America*, Boston, 1876, Vol. I, pp. 375–76.

and a feeling of remorse over the ill treatment of the Indians and Negroes.

During the early and middle decades of the nineteenth century, the philosophy of the French Enlightenment, together with the opportunities provided by the frontier, influenced American thought. For it was then that the belief in man's capabilities, spiritual and intellectual, promoted reform as well as economic development. But in the last third of the century, with the growth of monopoly, corruption and greater differences in living standard, a modified form of English Puritanism gained the upper hand. As the United States entered the present century, and the American promise fell far short of realization, Jeffersonian idealism tended to give way to Hamiltonian realism or even cynicism.

By 1920 the United States had emerged as the greatest world power, and with the highest living standards for her people. But due to the changing socio-economic structure, she presented a picture of frustration as well as of hope.

F. Major Expansive Societies in Asia: Japan and China, Their Similarities and Contrasts

Crossing the Pacific in 1890, we again visit Asia's principal expansive societies: Japan and China. In many respects, the two societies were strikingly similar. They had a common written language, a comparable religious background and family institutions which showed a marked resemblance. Moreover, their socio-political structures were alike. In each of the two societies there was an emperor, a corps of magistrates who took their directives from the capital, and a body of lesser officials who supervised local governments. In each, the magistrates and minor officials were usually chosen from the landed gentry. Furthermore, in each, those officials who also had served in a military capacity and risen in the ranks enjoyed considerable prestige; in fact, some were able to influence court policies. In Japan, from 1884, there was a cabinet responsible to the emperor and a bicameral legislature with restricted representation. But the most influential persons at cabinet meetings were the war and naval ministers, generals and admirals, all of whom had formerly been either court nobles or samurai. In China, those held in comparable esteem were the generals, civil governors, most of whom had served as army officers, and court mandarins.

These similarities were important, but there was also a significant difference between the two societies. Whereas Japanese of all classes upheld the expansive structure of their country, the Chinese peasantry, especially those living near the frontier, were inclined toward migratory social patterns and modes of thought. Hence, while the Japanese disciplined themselves on behalf of their state, many Chinese were, on occasions, in open rebellion. The fact that the Japanese, in contrast to the Chinese, practiced self-denial in support of their empire enabled them to achieve world power status by the end of the century.

Centering our attention first on Japan, we may trace the source of the self-denial among her people. We may recall that in Japan, centuries earlier, the conversion to Buddhism had eased the conscience of the Japanese upper class, just as the acceptance of Christianity had lessened the guilt feelings of the Roman and German. We may further recall that in both Europe and Asia an uprising against any hierarchy having a religious foundation promoted additional acts of self-denial to justify such an action. In northern Europe the aristocratic and burgher upheaval against the Roman pope and prelates led to self-privation on behalf of the state or of capitalistic enterprise. Similarly, in Japan, the veritable revolution of the warriors

against the court nobles—those closest to the much revered emperor—caused the former to undergo even further
privation than formerly, and for the benefit of the country. This they did from 1192, the year that their leader,
Minamoto Yoritomo, established his Bakufu (military
government) at Kamakura and assumed the title of
shogun (generalissimo).

During the succeeding centuries there were rulers and
cliques which deviated from the path of austerity, but
sooner or later they aroused stiff opposition from the ranks
of the warriors, most of whom continued to practice self-
control. For during the period of the Kyoto Bakufu
(1392-1615), the shoguns sought to rival the emperors
and erect splendid palaces and pavilions. But such pretension only created moral indignation and uprisings from
discontented bushi (warriors), and there commenced an
extended age of internal strife. From about 1470 to 1600,
feudal warfare was the order of the day.

In the late sixteenth century, however, three captains—
Oda Nobunaga, Hideyoshi Toyotomi, and Tokugawa
Iyeyasu—arose in succession to assume leadership. These
three generals maintained strict discipline within the
ranks of their armies and did much to bring unity to the
divided country. It was the third of the trio, Iyeyasu, who,
upon achieving final victory over his rivals, moved the
capital to Yedo (Tokyo) and founded the third Bakufu
(1616-1868).

At this time, the bushi were already divided horizon-
tally into daimyo (great names, or feudal lords) and samurai (their knightly retainers). But Iyeyasu also separated
them vertically into fudai (his immediate vassals) and
tozama (the outside lords). Toward the fudai, some of
whom were blood relations, he was rather indulgent. He
gave them considerable financial support through the
taxes collected from the farmers in their fiefs. Toward
the tozama the shogun held aloof. He refused to render

them any financial assistance, so that they had to depend upon their own resources.

The fudai daimyo, no longer independent lords but dependent vassals, became increasingly fond of luxuries. They and their samurai retainers purchased such luxury items as braided swords, ceremonial robes, silk garments, scrolls, and tapestries. They also acquired expensive tastes in food and alcohol. Furthermore, they indulged heavily in sexual pleasures. Why was there this drastic change in their manner of living? Because this was their way of compensating for the dependent role which they were compelled to assume. And in order to discourage rebellion the shogun requested all daimyo to make a journey to Yedo every other year, and upon returning, leave their wives and children in the capital as hostages.

The tozama, on their part, detested the shogun and fudai and wished to overthrow them. Still, in order to do so, they had to believe that they had moral sanction. They were already convinced that they had such sanction, at least in part. For in contrast to the fudai, they exercised far greater self-control. They ate and drank simply, avoided extravagance in dress and entertainment and, in general, abstained from other pleasures. Thus, they could observe the behavior of the hereditary vassals and look upon themselves as alone having retained the customary feudal virtues.[57]

However, living a more Spartan-like existence was not alone sufficient to justify a seizure of power from the shogun and fudai. Since the shogun enjoyed the confidence of the emperor, further means of justification were necessary. The theme which needed to be stressed was that centuries ago the shoguns had deprived the emperors of their rightful authority. Therefore, alongside the wish to remove the shogun, there arose the desire to restore the emperor.

---

57. Sansome, *Japan, A Short Cultural History*, p. 515.

Following the Meiji Restoration in 1868, the self-control and loyalty practiced by the samurai on behalf of their feudal lords were now maintained for the Imperial House. Loyalty and self-discipline were the watchwords of the tozama samurai who effected and profited by the Restoration. They continued to be the watchwords of the military class which, in the following century guided the ship of state.

In directing the affairs of state, the new elite of imperial officials and army and naval officers received ample popular support. For the common people, too, were taught to practice self-discipline and loyalty. The people not only paid the necessary taxes so that the government could subsidize industry and build up a huge defense force. They also acknowledged class distinctions, showing proper respect to those of higher station, the very use of language denoting one's relative status. Furthermore, with customary modesty, they generally refrained from expressing frank opinions, at least in public. As on middle-class social occasions in Britain and Germany, group singing was more popular and acceptable than candid conversation. Education was widespread, with a high rate of literacy as the result. Yet, throughout their school years, boys were encouraged not only to study hard, but to engage in such national sports as kendo (fencing) and judo. Girls were induced to learn tea ceremony and flower arrangement as suitable training for future matrimony.

From this description we could easily get the impression that Japanese society practiced extreme self-denial. In several respects, however, it was less self-denying than the British or the German. Punctuality, though appreciated in Japan, was not as much of a requirement, particularly on social occasions, as in northern Europe. Time was regarded as important, but certain hours were set aside for recreation. For instance, no plays, kabuki dramas, and banraku (puppet shows) were attended primarily for entertainment, the spectators consisting mainly of women and older people. As for men, indulgence in alcohol and in extramarital relations, while not accepted as proper by Japanese society, did not cause as deep a sense of guilt as they did in Protestant Europe. The allotment of special districts in the larger cities attested to a more lenient attitude, and pledges of university students to remain chaste were rare, if they existed at all. Thus, it could be said that the Japanese, though self-denying, were not rigidly so.

How was the expansive social structure and the general, though limited, practice of self-denial reflected in the country's literature? Since Japanese society was expansive, and the people were loyal to the political order, the outstanding fiction writers remained aloof from social questions. Instead, they tended to portray individual man's limitations. But while doing so, they did not castigate him, as did certain writers in the West. The reason for the milder attitude in Japan lay in the difference between Buddhism and Christianity. Both religions were pessimistic in their conception of human nature and their exponents were ever urging repentance. But whereas Christianity referred to man's "original sin" and "inherent evil," Buddhism merely maintained that man's nature is such as to lead to frustration and sorrow. In effect, Christianity surpassed Buddhism in its adverse criticism of humanity.

Because of the milder nature of Buddhism, the Japanese seldom went to the extreme of condemning man. Instead of castigating him, they pointed out defects, but with an air of pity. While offering no solution, they urged their readers to be sympathetic. During the Yedo era (1616-1868), Chikamatsu Monzaemon (1653-1724), "the Shakespeare of Japan," composed dramas in which the characters commit sins and meet with disaster; yet, the stress is not upon their evil deeds, but upon the hopelessness of the situation. The same was true in the works of the novelist, Ihara Saikaku (1624-1693). Here, the characters are weak and vacillating and get into difficulty, owing to an inherent lack of strength in their constitution.

The same tendency could be seen throughout the Meiji era (1868-1912). True, writers in Japan were influenced by several in the West, but then the particular Western writers would not have been able to impart ideas to the Japanese, had not the latter considered them plausible. The renowned novelist Natsume Soseki was highly impressed with the writings of George Meredith. The reason was that Meredith struck an impressive chord: the limitation and loneliness of man, as portrayed in *The Ordeal of Richard Feveral*. In *Botchan*, Natsume also stressed the difficulties which individuals have in understanding each other, while in *Kokoro,* he depicted the guilt feeling of a professor who, unintentionally, had done injury to a friend. The isolation of man was, likewise, a much emphasized theme of two other distinguished novelists: Mori Ogai and Futabatei Shimei.

The closely related idea that the average individual, at least, has a limited perspective was the subject of Japanese political theorists during the Meiji era and even later. One school maintained that the common people, having been oppressed during the long feudal period, were ignorant in the ways of politics and should be educated. Their leading spokesman was Itagaki Taisuke, a member of the Japanese Diet, who stated:

"Good governments depend on good people. Therefore, to reform the government and ensure lasting benefits from it, we should reform the national character and foster good people. We cannot hope for reform of the national character so long as the educated and the ignorant classes are so far apart in their understanding of politics as to lack a feeling of concord with each other. Therefore, our party should help the educated lead the ignorant and the ignorant to follow the educated onward, and thus spread political understanding and establish the welfare of the people on a sound foundation."[58]

Opposing this liberal school was another and very significant one. Like Pareto and his followers in Italy, this group contended that coup d'etats were, at times, necessary. For since the members of the Japanese Diet were elected from the general public, they were "incompetent" to give advice, let alone enact legislation, and should be replaced by an elite that possesses spirit and integrity. The leading exponent of this school was Yamagata Aritomo, a military official rather than a civilian, and he asserted:

"There must be several million, among our population of seventy million, who have fixed property and are economically secure, and who, therefore, are above corruption. If such men come forward to organize a solid nucleus in the Diet, the Empire will be on a firm and secure foundation, and there need be no anxiety in the country. The epoch-making task of establishing our sovereign and our country was accomplished by thousands of devoted and self-sacrificing patriots of the period prior to and after the Restoration. Today, firty years since the Restoration, when our national fortunes continue to rise, are there no patriots who would step forward to save our country from the dangers which are imminent? It is my fervent hope that such men will brace themselves to action."[59]

Generally, the consensus of Japanese intellectuals could be found between the opposing views expressed by Itagaki and Yamagata. For example, Nitobe Inazu, a nationalistic historian and interpreter of Japanese culture to the West, like his Western counterparts, also treated the problem of war and peace. While not condoning war in itself, Nitobe attempted to justify Japan's adventure in Manchuria on both moral and political grounds. In the

---

58. *Records of Civilization: Sources and Studies*, LIV, pp. 688–9.
59. *Ibid.*, pp. 713–14.

following excerpts from a series of lectures delivered during a trip to the United States, in 1932, he said:

"Our need of Manchuria, either for defense or for economic reasons, would not be sufficient in itself for military control. We ought to be able to adjust our relations with China in Manchuria in a peaceful, lawful way. Why do we resort to force?

"Candidly, what other resort is there under the circumstances? There is no stable government in China. Much of the country is in disorder. You who are far away and not deeply affected may remain indifferent, as we would if there should be disturbances in Nicaragua or Salvador. But China is our close neighbor, and her general state a matter of deep concern and, at times, of positive danger to us. We have many Japanese citizens living in that country. Their life and property are constantly menaced, and the Chinese government cannot protect them. Under the circumstances, you would, I believe, take action, and so must we."[60]

Generally, it could be said that since Japanese society was expansive, the leading writers of the country did not press for reform; since the people were loyal to the ruling circles, the authors did not seek revolution. At the same time, the practice of self-denial was somewhat tempered. Hence, the circumstances were not so rigid as to induce militant attitudes among most intellectuals and laymen. The lack of a widespread militancy could be seen during the war with China, in the 1930's, when the public, while loyally supporting the adventure, did so, it would seem, with only moderate enthusiasm.

Turning our attention from Japan to China, we come upon a rather different scene. Though both societies were expansive, the Chinese, generally, were less self-denying, a revolt against a class or person acknowledged as sacred, not having occurred in China as in Japan. To be sure,

60. Nitobe, *Lectures on Japan*, Tokyo, 1936, pp. 251-52.

there were periodic uprisings against the emperors in China, resulting in the ousting of one dynasty and the establishment of another. But the fact that there were so many dynastic changes is an indication that the Chinese emperors were not held in as deep a reverence as were the mikados in Japan or the popes in Europe. The reason is that from early times, a Chinese dynasty owed its success in securing the throne to secular, indeed military, rather than spiritual leadership. Accordingly, the position of emperor, in China, depended less upon religious sanction than was the case with the Japanese mikado or the Roman pontiff.

The relative lack of self-denial among the Chinese affected all classes. The upper class, composed mainly of gentlemen farmers rather than military landowners, had little sense of obligation to either court or peasantry. They were loyal to a dynasty only as long as it could protect them and safeguard their interests; if it showed signs of weakness, they did nothing to sustain it. Any true loyalty on their part was to family or clan.

Toward the peasants, the gentry had little of the paternalism that one found in feudal Japan. Hence, the Chinese peasant lived and worked amid greater hardship and with less security than did his Japanese counterpart. Invariably, the peasant had to pay for the sumptuous feasts and all night gambling sessions that were frequently held by the squire. Hence, it was the peasant who groaned under the weight of high rent, heavy taxation or land hunger. If he could pay increased rent, his tax burden would be lighter, since the landlord would then shoulder some of the payments due the State. But if, as in times of flood or drought, the peasant, faced with a poor harvest, was unable to pay either the rent or the tax, he would be evicted from the land. As a consequence, he would wander to the nearest town and become a coolie, or, if failing to find work, would move to the frontier and turn to banditry.

The peasant in China had not always been faced with such a severe plight. We may recall that during the much earlier Hsia (2205-1766 B.C.) and Shang (1766-1122 B.C.) dynasties, and in the first half of the Chou (1122-255 B.C.), the peasants, while regarded as an inferior class, had, nevertheless, been assured of their status as tenants. This was arranged through a system known as the Tsing Tien, by which a section of land was apportioned among nine households.[61] The idea in support of this arrangement was migratory: since each family is an integral part of the village, it is entitled to use the land. Later, the system suffered from feudalistic abuses, and it finally was abolished by the first emperor (246-210 B.C.). Admittedly, during the Ts'in Dynasty (265-420 A.D.), the Emperor Wang Mang tried to reintroduce it in order to cure China of her economic illness; in the Sung (976-1127) the minister, Wang-an-Shih, made similar attempts. But in these endeavors they were opposed by the powerful landlord class and its friends at court. Yet, while the Tsing Tien system was discarded by the court, local magistrates and gentry, memory of it was kept alive by the peasants who had migrated to China's extensive frontier. Here, China resembled Russia.

In defending the later arrangement whereby a landlord could evict his tenant at will, the court and gentry referred to the teachings of Confucius. This most esteemed of all Chinese sages had taught that one should respect his peers merely because of their superior position in society. Therefore the peasants should behave kindly toward their landlords, even if the latter were charging high rent, or were about to evict them, and, hence, didn't merit such kindness.

But while the upper class relied upon Confucianism to justify its policies, the discontented peasants sought consolation in Taoism. For the Taoists denounced any form

---

61. Lee, *The Economic History of China*, pp. 35–44.

of social hierarchy and stood solidly for equality. In an earlier chapter, I indicated that the Taoist preacher and author, Chuang Tzu, believed that no one in society should have more than a certain share of the total wealth. He should be neither rich nor poor, exalted nor degraded, and even if having attained the rank of minister or emperor, he should never make others feel as if they were in low station.

The Taoist teachings, as taught by Chuang Tzu, appealed to the intellect and, as such, attracted many writers and scholars. Though these intellectual adherents were critical of the Chinese social system, they did not advocate its overthrow through violence. But when, a century or more after Chuang Tzu's time, the creed was imparted to the peasants, and especially to those who had migrated to the frontier, it was transformed. The earlier rationalism and mild social criticism gave way to a belief in magic, visions of utopia, and demands for revolution. The Taoist priests on the frontier not only preached complete equality; they also assured the peasants that through the use of magic formulas they could invoke the aid of the nature gods in removing the gentry.

The peasants and bandits responded willingly to these assurances, and, accordingly, Taoists became leaders of armed uprisings. Such, for example, was the occasion with the Yellow Turban revolt, which erupted at the close of the Eastern Han Dynasty (32-220 A.D.). Such was also probable in the case of the Huang Ch'ao uprising, at the end of the Tang Dynasty (618-907); the Fang La rebellion, toward the close of the Sung (976-1127); or the Li Tsu-cheng and Chang Hsien-chung revolts, in the last years of the Ming (1368-1644).

Indeed, almost every major revolt was prompted by a religious cult, Taoist or other, whose teachings had, at least, migratory overtones. This was perhaps even more true in the nineteenth than in the preceding centuries, for with the lapse of time migratory sentiment grew even stronger. This was the case with the Nien Fei uprising, which began in Honan and spread to the coastal province of Anhui. It was especially the occasion with the even more formidable Taiping rebellion, which originated in Hupei, raged along the Yangtze eastward, and then northward to the Yellow River, before it was suppressed. The program of the Taiping leaders contained the following significant clauses:

"All the land in the country is to be cultivated by the whole population together. If there is an insufficiency [of land] in this place, move some of the people to another place. . . . All lands in the country are also to be mutually supporting with respect to abundance and scarcity. If this place has a drought, then draw upon the abundant harvest elsewhere in order to relieve the distress here. . . . Thus, all the people of the country may enjoy the great blessings of the Heavenly Father, Supreme Ruler and Lord-God on High."[62]

The rules concerning relations between the sexes are also noteworthy, in that they resembled those of the ancient Greek and Roman cults:

"When one first creates a new rule, the state must come first and the family last, public interests first and private interests last. Moreover, as it is advisable to avoid suspicion (of improper conduct) between the inner (female) and the outer (male) and to distinguish between male and female, so men must have male quarters and women must have female quarters; only thus can we be dignified and avoid confusion. There must be no common mixing of the male and female groups, which would cause debauchery and violation of Heaven's commandments."[63]

Here, an emerging migratory pattern, with its planned economy, strict morality and adherence to a theocratic

62. *Records of Civilization: Sources and Studies,* LV, p. 694.
63. *Ibid.,* pp. 703–04.

order, is highly evident. The sense of cohesion among those participating in the rebellion was actually strengthened by their espousal of a near Christian monotheism rather than of the earlier Taoist polytheism.

Migratory sentiment continued to make inroads in the nineteenth century, and among China's intellectuals as well as peasants. To complete the emerging migratory thought pattern, all that was needed was an in-group concept, in which China was regarded as highly distinguishable from other societies. This missing link was provided, at the turn of the century, by a group of nationalistic, though progressive, scholars. One such scholar was Liang Ch'i-chao, who had studied abroad, but returned to China convinced that his country had a unique culture which should, by all means, be preserved. This view he set forth in an essay entitled "A People Made New." He wrote:

"Our people have been established as a nation on the Asian continent for several thousand years, and we must have some special characteristics which are grand, noble and perfect, and distinctly different from those of other races. We should preserve these characteristics and not let them be lost."[64]

In the manner of Tolstoi and Dostoevsky, Liang Ch'i-chao emphasized the differences between his country and the foreign societies, a truly migratory outlook. Yet, this outlook should not be confused with the expansive view that all foreign states are vassals of the "Celestial Kingdom," a view held in Chinese court circles. Nor was it the same as the belief of Japanese officials that it was their mission to rule and educate the people on the Asian mainland.

Thus, a survey of modern Japan and China up to the Second World War shows an integrated expansive society alongside one that was disintegrated. It reveals a Japan whose socio-political system was that of a hierarchy, but whose subjects, in thought and deed, rendered it sufficient

---

64. *Ibid.*, p. 756.

support. True, there was some difference of opinion among Japanese scholars. Still, in general, they supported the established order, almost the only liberal sentiment being in the nature of a request for greater political education.

The survey also shows a China whose ruling class had changed but little during the transition from monarchy to republic. For despite the good intentions of Dr. Sun Yat-sen, there remained at the Chinese political helm the tradition-conscious magistrates, gentry and warlords. This fact, together with the persistence of a migratory tradition on the frontier and the absence of a philosophy of conformity throughout China, rendered revolutionary the Chinese peasants, workers and writers, thus paving the way for a dynamic upheaval.

G. Imperalism: A Study in Comparative Colonial Policy

So far in our discussion, we have related the comparative attitudes of the different societies toward the questions of war, conquest and the role and status of the common people. As judged by the opinions of the philosophers and writers—the most sensitive and circumspect element in a society—the attitudes have varied from one country to another. A more humane outlook has been evident in societies which have been interactive; a more ruthless perspective, in those which have been expansive. A society which has been interactive and, at the same time, rather tolerant of self-gratification has been most humane; one that has been expansive and also rigidly self-denying has been least.

At present, the problem which now concerns us is how the European, American and Asian societies have reacted to the question of imperialism. What have been their attitudes toward subject peoples, and how have these attitudes influenced colonial policy? From our preceding discussion, we would expect that while all the major expansive, and also interactive, societies have had colonial empires—Russia and China excepted—their attitudes have varied. Generally, the expansive societies have conquered, at times, with directness and vigor, especially if their upper classes have felt deprived of the opportunity to have done so in the past. For with such deprivation, the aristocracies or military orders have felt that they were losing their raison d'etre. The interactive societies, on the other hand, having had plutocratic rather than military and aristocratic elites, have been more or less apologetic after acquiring new territories. For not having the sense of *noblesse oblige,* the bourgeois elites have, in building empires, assumed a somewhat unnatural role. Generally, therefore, the interactive societies, having been apologetic, have been more liberal in their colonial policies than have the expansive. Moreover, the societies practicing self-denial in greater degree have, in several respects, been more rigid in their colonial rule than have those with a more relaxed attitude toward daily conduct.

First, we will consider the imperialistic attitudes and policies of the earliest expansive societies in modern Europe: Portugal and Spain. Then, we will turn our attention to the interactive: the Netherlands, Belgium, the United Kingdom, France, and the United States. Finally, we will discuss the very recent expansive states: Italy, Japan, and Germany.

In the fifteenth and sixteenth centuries, Spain and Portugal were the very creation of expansion, an expansion which had been undertaken against the Moors, three hundred years earlier. This aggression had been in the nature of an anti-Moslem crusade. Its leaders had been nobles and knights from southern France and northern Iberia, and in their push southward, these aristocratic warriors had strengthened their hold upon the emerging Spanish and Portuguese societies. By the fifteenth century, Spain and Portugal had each become unified states, and their lesser nobles—knights and captains—then embarked upon a series of overseas conquests. Ostensibly, the conquests were for the purpose of spreading the Catholic faith, but the real motive of the lesser nobles in these exploits was to justify their position in society. For if they could prove that they were capable of subjugating, regardless of the welfare of those subjugated, they merited their social rank.

Portuguese and Spanish rule was typical of that implemented by certain of the ancient expansive states. In the Malay Peninsula, Angola, Mozambique, and Brazil, the Portuguese administrators governed without much regard for the wishes of the natives; local and tribal self-government were virtually nonexistent. They also had little concern for the wellbeing of the subject peoples. They granted huge tracts of land to Portuguese settlers and, with them, control over the inhabitants living on them. They levied poll taxes which the natives could hardly pay, and which compelled the latter to seek work on plantations that were owned by the settlers. The Portuguese were among the first to introduce the slave trade, and it is said that the life of a Brazilian slave was usually from seven to ten years.[65]

The picture in the Spanish territories of Mexico, Peru, and the Philippines was equally grim. The rulers from Spain also allotted entire districts to settlers; they, too, imposed exorbitant taxes; they, likewise, had servile labor; indeed, the corvee in Mexico and Peru was notorious for its high mortality rate.

Perhaps the only favorable aspect of Portuguese and Spanish imperialism was the fact that the Iberians did not draw the color line too rigidly. Intermingling, or even intermarriage, between Spanish or Portuguese males and Indian or Negro females was frequent. There emerged

---

65. C. R. Boxer, *Race Relations in the Portuguese Colonial Empire*, Oxford, 1963, p. 101.

large numbers of mestizos and mulattoes, some of them securing high positions in the colonial militia or in the Church, others becoming rich through the slave trade. Yet, regardless of wealth or position, the mixed bloods were never accepted as social equals by the Iberian colonists.

During the three centuries of Spanish and four centuries of Portuguese rule, the colonial policies and practices improved only slightly. Almost the only indication of better conditions was the abolition of slavery by 1900. However, the ban on human cargo was due largely to the pressure of public opinion in the interactive societies.

Why was Portuguese and Spanish policy so ruthless? For one thing, there was the zeal for conquest found among knights and army captains in expansive societies, and which induced little consideration for those subjugated. For another, there was the tyranny of the Inquisition, a tyranny which was stifling and conducive to cruelty, when the opportunity arose.

When we pass from the early modern expansive to the interactive colonial powers, the question may arise as to whether the latter, with their extensive empires, were not actually expansive societies. Nevertheless, despite their annexation of foreign territories, the Netherlands, Belgium, Great Britain, France, and the United States were interactive, and not expansive, as I defined the terms at the outset. Then, I indicated that a society was expansive if its power structure and mode of thought was derived from the very act of expansion. By the same token, a society was interactive if its thought and structure were derived from interaction; or migratory if its organization and ideas showed the imprint of a migration, even in the remote past. Hence, in the late modern period, what matters is not necessarily the extent of the land acquired by the particular society but rather the nature of its socio-political structure and social thought. For even though these five societies had overseas empires, their influential classes

were still composed mainly of bourgeoisie, their governments continued to be parliamentarian, their value systems, those of merchants, bankers and industrialists and
their sentiments, those of reform.

Turning first to the Dutch empire in Indonesia, we note
that here the policy of the colonial administrators was
milder than that in the Spanish and Portuguese possessions. This was due to the interactive nature of Dutch
society and to the absence of an Inquisition in Holland.
But while Dutch colonial policy was not nearly as ruthless
as the Portuguese or Spanish, it was not particularly humane. Being enterprising business men and good Calvinists, the Dutch East India Company directors were
intent on making the colony pay. Hence, they established
huge plantations for the purpose of cultivating exportable
crops. They also caused what had been a meager money
economy to become widespread. Owing to these innovations, the rice-farming Indonesian peasants were faced
with higher prices and compelled to borrow. Failing to
meet their obligations, many were forced by circumstances
to work on the Dutch-owned plantations, and the village
economy was undermined.

In the nineteenth century, the administration of Indonesia became the responsibility of the Dutch government.
With this transfer of control, there was an effort to protect the natives from exploitation; also, a measure of self-
government was granted. However, these apologetic moves
were partly offset by the policy of admitting only Indonesian nobles to the colonial civil service.[66] For Calvinism,
with its tendency to place persons in categories according
to their alleged degree of godliness, was slow in removing
social barriers.

In some respects, the history of Indonesia under Dutch
rule compared with that of the Congo under the Belgian

66. H. W. Sundstrom, *Indonesia: Its People and Politics,* Tokyo, 1957,
pp. 59–62.

government. The Congo venture, first organized as a company enterprise under King Leopold II and leading stockholders, was the scene of vicious exploitation. Although there wasn't slavery in the Congo—indeed, the Arab slave dealers were ousted from the region by the Belgians—the natives were forced to deliver a certain quota of rubber and ivory or face punishment. Soon public opinion in Belgium, Britain, France, and the United States compelled the company to relinquish control to the Belgian government. Under governmental supervision conditions improved. Here, however, the comparison with Dutch rule is significant. For while granting little in the way of self-government and still demanding some, though much lighter, quotas, the Belgians did not uphold a caste system.

Turning our attention from Dutch and Belgian to British colonial policy, we notice a certain similarity. The British, too, were motivated by the desire to promote business and withal a flourishing trade between the mother country and their vast overseas possessions. In India, Burma, and Malaysia, they, too, set up large private establishments alongside native villages, where the inhabitants lived and worked by traditional rules. They, too, introduced a money economy and, subsequently, industrial workshops, thereby disrupting the village organizations and native crafts. In South and East Africa, they made use of a poll tax to compel the tribesmen to work in the mines. Throughout Africa they also imposed a color bar; in this, they resembled the Boers in the south.

Still, the British, in like manner, were hardly as cruel as the Iberians. To be sure, they engaged in the slave trade but yet were the first to abolish it; they even patrolled the high seas to make sure that the ban on human cargo was enforced. They allowed the native princes and chiefs a major share in local government; for affairs concerning the territory as a whole, they established legislative councils with native representation. As far as possible, they (as did the Dutch and Belgians) introduced methods of sanitation. Finally, they protected their possessions from marauders and invaders, and such protection contributed greatly to population growth. Indeed, Lord Macaulay, a leading apologist for British overseas expansion, justified Britain's rule over India by stating that it had brought peace and security to the inhabitants.[67]

With respect to policies and practices in her colonial empire, Britain, in general, resembled France. In Indo-China and North Africa, the economic changes introduced by French rule were comparable to those which transpired in the British and Dutch empires. There were also the replacement of a barter by a money economy, the growth of extensive plantations and the threat to village institutions.

However, the French, being even more apologetic than the British and Dutch in having acquired such a vast domain, were still milder in their imperialism. In fact, one colonial minister, Jacques Stern, contended that France, in contrast to the other colonial powers, never imposed her special legislation and administrative system on the people in her colonies, but tried to understand their customs and sentiments.[68] While this was an overstatement, there was some measure of truth in it. In the French empire, alongside the progress made in sanitation, there was no forced labor and little in the way of coercion in the matter of cultivating exportable crops. Then too, all natives were treated as French citizens, and there was frequent association between them and the civil servants sent from Paris. An American author on Southeast Asia commented that whereas the British officials maintained a formal dignity in their dealings with the natives and

---

67. Macaulay, "Government of India," in *Speeches on Politics and Literature*.
68. J. Stern, *The French Colonies: Past and Future*, New York, 1944, p. 39.

remained aloof from them, the French were inclined to fraternize.[69] This inclination of the French was consistent with their practice of not drawing the color line.

The more apologetic attitude of the French is to be attributed to their background. Since the French Revolution, France's social structure conformed more readily to the interactive pattern than did Britain's, and this despite periods of reaction. Since 1875, the French political structure did so as well. True, in contrast to Britain, there were threats to the republic from disgruntled generals. But throughout the republican era, there was never a *coup d'état*, though the recent change from the Fourth to the Fifth Republic was effected in order to prevent one.

As the French were more interactive and, as we have noted, relaxed in their manner of living, they did not have as great an urge to build an empire, and their leading intellectuals were indifferent to, if not opposed to, overseas expansion. In fact, in acquiring an empire, French statesmen and bourgeoisie were motivated more by the desire to have available a source of manpower in the event of a war with Germany than by a wish to foster trade. At the same time, there was hardly a sense of *noblesse oblige* that would have induced conquest as a justification for status in society; nor was there as widespread an urge to be successful in business enterprise as there was in other interactive societies. Indeed, the comparative freedom from self-denial in France allowed for a more fraternal attitude toward colonial peoples.

When turning from the colonial policies of Britain and France to those of the United States, we observe a blending of British, French, and American attitudes toward native peoples. In the Philippines (prior to independence), Samoa, Guam, Hawaii, and Puerto Rico, the American administrators refrained from policies of coer-

69. John Cady, *Southeast Asia: Its Historical Development*, New York, 1964, p. 432.

cion, while allowing a money economy and extensive plantations to flourish. Also, American officials were on more cordial terms with the people of these countries than were the British with their subjects, while, at the same time, they prepared them for self-government. The Puritan spirit of business enterprise and respect for parliamentary institutions were indicative of British and coastal American influence; the tendency to be informal when dealing with native inhabitants indicated a frontier American and French impact.

Moreover, in the United States, as in France and to a lesser extent in Britain, there were protests against imperialism. Progressives, such as William James, and conservatives, like William Graham Sumner, were alike in condemning the acquisition of the Philippines and Puerto Rico, in the wake of the Spanish-American War. Indeed, there is little question that the United States was reluctant to establish a widespread overseas empire.

Completing our tour of the colonial empires and considering finally those of the recent expansive societies—Italy, Japan, and Germany—we find generally less consideration shown to subject peoples than in the interactive possessions; in fact, Nazi German imperialism was outright oppression. But before discussing the imperialistic policies of these three societies, it would be well to explain briefly the political changes they underwent between the two world wars.

We well know that the political systems which were established in Italy, Japan, and Germany in the decades of the 1920's and '30's were those of fascism, militarism, and Nazism, respectively. But what was the underlying cause of their establishment, indeed, of the movements themselves? The fundamental cause was the discontent of the lower middle classes in these countries. Being mostly small independent or tenant farmers, shopkeepers, and clerical workers, these members of the lower middle class felt that since they were not ordinary proletarians they had a stake in society. They even aspired to higher positions or to better means of income. Yet, while having these aspirations, they found that in expansive societies the path to "success" was usually barred. Almost invariably, the only way they could scale the economic and social ladder was through intermarriage or by rapid promotion in military or government service.

There was little question of their resentment at having so little opportunity to improve their condition. The resentment of the lower middle classes was subconsciously directed toward the aristocratic elites, and even more toward the upper middle classes of well to do gentry and haut bourgeoisie. But owing to their educational background, which stressed loyalty to pope, emperor, or state, as well as to their being property-owners or small shareholders, they could not become revolutionists. Instead, they diverted their hostility into what were more socially accepted channels. They directed their antagonism toward alleged enemies of the pope, emperor, or state, at home or abroad. Thus imbued with nationalism, the more ambitious among them proceeded to organize.

It is significant that these newly established nationalistic organizations drew their largest following from the rural regions. For it was here that loyalty to spiritual ruler, temporal sovereign or nation was most strongly emphasized. Thus, in Italy the majority of those who made up the Fascist militia were from the agrarian south and central area rather than from the industrial north. In Japan, the ultranationalistic army officers, who comprised a distinct and influential circle, were usually from the rural Tohoku region in the northeast. In Germany, the Nazi leaders drew their heaviest vote and largest number of recruits from the Prussian hinterland, the stronghold of German Lutheranism.[70]

---

70. Frederick L. Schumann, *Hitler and the Nazi Dictatorship*, London, 1936, p. 145.

These movements gained in momentum as the states themselves tried to cope with economic crises. Amid the confusion, the ultranationalists secured the support of the elites in their respective countries, and with the latters' assistance were able to seize the political reins. Hence, in Italy, Mussolini and his Fascisti were appointed to leadership by the king, court, and military-industrial clique. In Japan, Viscount Saito and other right-wing leaders gained the ascendancy through the help of the landowning elite and bureaucracy. In Germany, Hitler and his Nazi party were able to obtain control through the connivance of the Junker officials, for the Junkers comprised the ruling circle of the Weimar Republic, just as they did that of the preceding imperial regime. Once in power, the Fascists, militarists, and Nazis were able to lend strength to the expansive societies, of which they were definite elements.

It might be argued that since these militant groups were mainly from the lower middle class, their political ascendancy marked at least partial transitions from expansive to interactive societies. However, the significant fact is that even before they were given the political reins, these disgruntled members of the petit bourgeois and peasant class never really identified themselves with that class, for to do so would have meant that they were revolutionists. Instead, they sought identification with the state. After their ascendance to power, the Fascists, militarists, and Nazis continued to identify themselves with their respective states, and this entailed cooperation with the older expansive hierarchies. The cooperation was there, even though the hierarchies appeared to play only passive roles in formulating domestic and foreign policies.

It was in the interests of the older hierarchies that their nations embark upon courses of expansion. Also, that it was a lofty and noble policy to undertake such imperialistic ventures was the conviction of those who headed the new regimes in Italy, Japan, and Germany. Hence, the Italian adventure in East Africa; the Japanese, in the East Asian mainland; the German, in much of Europe.

Alongside these similarities among the Axis powers, there were also marked differences with respect to imperialistic practice. The Italian policy was milder than the Japanese, which, in turn, was harsh but hardly as cruel as the Nazi German. In Tripoli and later in Ethiopia, the Fascist administrators, to be sure, granted huge concessions to Italian companies and encouraged colonization from Italy on a grand scale. They also deprived the natives of self-government. At the same time, they did promote fraternization with Moslem brotherhoods and sought their advice on colonial matters. In Korea and later in Manchuria, the officials from Japan likewise granted extensive allotments to Japanese zaibatsu, or mergers, Then too, they not only forbid the Koreans and Manchurians to exercise the right of self-government, but made no attempt to fraternize.

Still, for an example of outright cruelty and sadism in dealing with conquered peoples, we must turn to the Nazis. It is ludicrous to speak of the Nazis in occupied Europe as having given land in abundance to cartels and deprived the people under their jurisdiction of self-government. For particularly characteristic of Nazi rule was the imposition of a caste system, in which the Germans were at the head of the pyramid, followed by other "Teutons," and then "Latins" and, last of all, Slavs and Jews. With the other "Teutons" the Nazis attempted fraternization, but without success. For the "Latins" they devised a system of compulsory service in factories and mines, while for the Slavs and Jews they imposed a regimen of slave labor, followed by systematic extermination.

Why, we may ask, was Italian policy milder than the Japanese, and neither as cruel as the Nazi German? The answer lies in the habits and customs of the conquerors themselves, that is, in the degree to which they practiced self-denial. The more rigid their way of life the greater the frustration and inner hostility of those who later served as administrators in the conquered countries. Already, we noted that the Italians were more leisurely in their daily habits than were the Japanese, and that both peoples were more tolerant of self-gratification than were the Germans, especially the Prussians. For in none of the twentieth-century colonial powers, except Britain and the Netherlands, was the Puritan conscience and spirit of self-denial as strong as it was in Prussia. But then neither Britain nor the Netherlands was an expansive society: Neither was dominated by an aristocratic hierarchy, nor did either have as rigid a system of class distinctions. Moreover, neither the British nor the Dutch were as subservient to government officials as were the people in Prussia.

In effect, a brief survey of colonial history reveals a decided difference in policy. While, at times, it is difficult to speak of a "mild" as against a "ruthless" imperialism, and while there were abuses in every empire, malpractice was still a matter of considerable degree. Abuses were manifold in the Portuguese, Spanish, and Nazi German empires, less prevalent in the Dutch, Belgian, Italian, and Japanese empires, and least so in the British (after the abolition of the slave trade), the American, and the French. Most significantly, the survey seems to indicate that the more frustrated and, hence, inwardly hostile an element of society is, the greater its cruelty to others when the opportunity arises.

H. World War, The Eclipse of the Expansive Societies and Emergence of the Neo-Migratory

From the preceding chapters, we saw that the expansive societies surpassed the interactive, not in the extent of foreign territory acquired, but, it would seem, in being imperialistic without pangs of conscience. For the blatant imperialism and warlike assertiveness of the expansive society was due to its very nature and to the special character of its ruling class. The members of this elite were constantly obsessed with the urge to display military prowess and, thereby, prove that they merited their rank in the social hierarchy. Such display was made principally to impress those in the strata below them. Usually, feats of arms were intended for the purpose of maintaining the loyalty and support of those in the middle and lower classes, but of the same nationality. At times, however, they had as their motive the discouragement of rebellion by subject peoples.

That both intentions—the maintaining of loyalty and discouragement of rebellion—could easily be sources of conflict was aptly illustrated by the First World War. This struggle was perpetrated mainly by Austria-Hungary, Russia, and Germany. Both Austria-Hungary and Russia were virtually governed by landed nobilities. Both aristocracies felt that military glory alone would sustain their regimes in the face of an uprising by Slavic subjects in the one empire, and by native peasants and workers in the other. Germany, while far more stable than the other two societies, nevertheless, had a proud Junker class, which was ever wary of losing its prestige. Such a loss would have made the rising class of industrialists, rather than itself, the power behind the Hohenzollern throne.

It may be argued that these three expansive societies were not chiefly responsible for the outbreak of war, but that the interactive States were equally provocative. However, the facts do not seem to warrant this conclusion. For example, just prior to the commencement of hostilities, the German government demanded that the French surrender the fortresses of Toul and Verdun as assurance of France's neutrality. On the other hand, the French government, even after issuing a call for mobilization, gave strict orders to the army forbidding any violation of German territory.[71] The comparative roles of the expansive and interactive societies, in this conflict, can be further illustrated. In the United Kingdom, parliament acted after Belgian neutrality had been violated, but the ruling clique in Italy entered the war without any provocation whatsoever from the Central Powers.

The urge to justify or maintain status, in an expansive society, was also the prime cause of the Second World War. The only difference was that in this last conflict it was the disgruntled lower middle classes of Italy, Japan, and Germany which obtained the political mantle. In this, they were ably assisted by the court, former samurai and Junkers, respectively, all of whom likewise had dreams of grandeur. For victory at arms would have bolstered the regimes and assured the status of both the older and newer scions of power. The result was the most destructive war in history.

In the pre-Industrial Age, military adventures could be undertaken with far less peril to the society concerned. For then, except for the Hundred Years and Thirty Years wars, conflicts were not nearly as devastating. But in the present century, and with the huge strides made in science and industry, it was a different matter. So destructive were the two world wars that defeat on the battlefield was felt far more than in days past. Accordingly, the expansive social structure, with its value system founded on military victory, faced a death warrant if having lost a war. And with defeat in the world wars, this is what transpired.

The past fifty years or more saw the eclipse of the leading expansive societies. World War I saw the fall of the Russian empire, which was already in the throes of a dynamic upheaval. It also saw the disintegration of the Austro-Hungarian and Ottoman imperial structures into petty expansive states, Czechoslovakia alone becoming in-

---

71. Alfred Cobban, *A History of Modern France* (Penguin), 1965, vol. III, p. 102.

teractive. World War II witnessed the demise of the Italian empire, the German empire (revived through Nazism) and the Japanese imperial state edifice. It further witnessed revolution within the already disintegrated Chinese empire.

These expansive societies were replaced by those that, at present, are either interactive or neo-migratory. I use the term "neo-migratory" in referring to the present-day communistic societies, because, in contrast to the earlier migratory, they, and Russia most notably, have entered the Industrial and Scientific Age.

The question as to whether the expansive society would be discarded for an interactive or a neo-migratory one was determined by potent forces which were well at work beneath the surface. It was hardly an accident that the coastal societies became interactive, and the larger and inland ones, neo-migratory. Generally, only smaller and coastal states, such as Italy, Germany, and Japan, could maintain capitalistic economies and bourgeois communities that, if free from aristocratic influence, would foster interactive societal patterns. On the contrary, usually only extensive and inland countries like Russia and China could have peasant communities that would wish to uphold the collectivistic economies and village organizations —the migratory patterns—which, while just partially existent in the present age, had been characteristic of the rural scene centuries earlier.

In Italy, West Germany, and Japan, since the end of World War II, the main characteristics of interactive societies have emerged. Military cliques and aristocracies have given way to bourgeois democracies, government by parliaments has replaced government by oligarchies and the martial system of values has been discarded for one which is more acceptable to commercial middle classes. There has been greater mobility from class to class; workers and farmers have far more freedom of expression, as also do those who own or manage the means of mass communication. A virtual individualism has become the order of the day, but, as in other interactive societies, it is an individualism which exists alongside requests for reform.

However, a rising interactive pattern has hardly been the occasion in Russia and China, following the collapse of their expansive edifices. For in these two countries there was a sparcity of bourgeois communities and, with it, a weakness in middle class sentiment. Previously, we noted that Russia had had little opportunity to be influenced by the urban and commercial revolutions, and by a renaissance or reformation. The case was similar in China. For China, also, was too vast and isolated for interactive processes to have gotten underway and promoted trade and urbanization on a wide scale. In China, too, there was little opportunity for the development of a humanistic literature, whose authors would have imparted the idea that the individual is worthy of consideration, apart from his family or clan. Equally important, in Chinese history, was the absence of a movement against a religious or semi-religious establishment, such as had occurred in northern Europe and Japan, respectively. For then, the discontented elements in China did not feel it to be their duty to practice self-denial on behalf of the state or the social order and, consequently, suppress their feelings.

Rather than the bourgeois community, it was the peasant village which was the bond of cohesion. It was to the village—the *mir* in Russia and the *tsien* in China—that the majority of people felt responsible. It was the village patriarchs or elders who supervised community affairs and were even the custodians of morality. From this standpoint, a near migratory pattern prevailed in the Russian and Chinese hamlet.

Alongside their ties to others in the village, family or clan, the peasants had a deeply rooted antagonism to the pillars of the expansive society: the gentry and the government. In Russia and China alike, the peasants considered the land as being theirs, at least collectively, and by traditional right; thus, they looked upon the gentry as usurpers. They further regarded the ruling circles as being of little help to them in their plight. It seemed as though the sole functions of the government were to collect taxes, uphold the privileges of the landlords, and punish those who protested.

With such mass fomentation occurring beneath the surface, little was needed to set off the explosion. More than enough was provided by a world war, with all the misery it entailed. The revolutions themselves were but the climaxes to processes that had been at work for generations. The Russian Revolution was the culmination of such outbreaks as Pugachev's rebellion; the Chinese Revolution was the recurrence of the Taiping rebellion, but on a grand scale.

From the time that the new regimes were established, the dominant patterns have been neo-migratory. Both the Soviet Union and Mainland China have been governed by their respective Communist parties. But the parties, in turn, are elites of veritable patriarchs. For it is they who imbue the people with the doctrines of the state and supervise their daily activities. Supervision is exercised with respect to both public and private life. It is apparent in the school, the factory, and the office; it is present in the home and in the centers of culture and recreation.

A cardinal principle of the new societies is that individual learning and achievement are alone insignificant; what is important is their contribution to the state. Indeed, the individual is taught that from the very moment of his birth, he is indebted to the society which reared and educated him. As we well know, work in Russia and China is a collective enterprise, since most property is state-owned and production and distribution state-supervised. Family life and even sexual morals are also evaluated according to their impact on society. In the early days of the Russian Revolution, Lenin said the following concerning indulgence:

"The revolution demands concentration, increase of forces. From the masses, from individuals. It cannot tolerate orgiastic conditions, such as are normal for the decadent heroes and heroines of D'Annunzio. Dissoluteness in sexual life is bourgeois, is a phenomenon of decay. The proletariat is a rising class. It doesn't need intoxication as a narcotic or a stimulus. Intoxication as little by sexual exaggeration as by alcohol. . . . It receives the strongest urge to fight from a class situation, from the communist ideal. It needs clarity, clarity, and again clarity. And so I repeat, no weakening, no waste, no destruction of forces. Self-control, self-discipline, not slavery, not even in love."[72]

Thus, Lenin's dire concern with regard to indulgence was due to a fear that it would sap the energy needed to build the new society. Such apprehension was comparable to that of very early societies where men abstained for fear that otherwise they would impair their ability to hunt or engage in battle.

In effect, even private and personal matters are the concern of the community, or more properly, of the commune. The identity of the individual with the commune was set forth by Stalin in a conversation with H. G. Wells:

"There neither is nor should be an irreconcilable contrast between the individual and the collective, between the interests of the individual personally and those of the collective. There should be none, for as much as collectivism—socialism—does not deny individual interests; it amalgamates them with the interests of the collective."[73]

---

72. Clara Zetkin, *Reminiscences of Lenin*, London, 1929, pp. 49–51.
73. Julian Towster, "Vyshinsky's Concept of Collectivity," in *Continuity and Change in Russian and Soviet Thought*. Cambridge, Harvard University Press, 19?

A similar view was expressed by Mao Tse-tung, not long after the completion of the Chinese Revolution:

"Individualism depicts the self-seeking that belongs to the road of the bourgeoisie. It epitomizes the culmination of the idealistic world outlook, the bourgeois standpoint and the counterrevolutionary attitude in general."[74]

In conclusion, the present-day neo-migratory societies are similar in organization and outlook to the earlier migratory and constitute a challenge to the way of life upheld in the interactive nations.

---

74. John W. Lewis, *Leadership in Communist China*, Ithaca, N.Y., Cornell University Press, 1963, pp. 62–63.

6
Conclusion

In our brief survey of world history, we have placed societies into several categories. First of all, we have divided them into migratory, interactive, and expansive, each having distinctive characteristics. We have distinguished the one type of society from the other two by noting the socio-political structures, attitudes toward the out-group and attendant systems of thought.

The migratory, or the neo-migratory of the present time, have had firm social solidarity in which individuals have been nearly anonymous members of collectivities; they have been governed by elites of patriarchs who have been both political and religious or quasi-religious leaders; and they have been suspicious of out-groups. The authors representing migratory communities or neo-migratory societies have contended that their in-groups surpass the out-group in purity and virtue and, through teaching or indoctrination, could set an example as to the correct way of life.

The interactive have allowed greater individual expression and right of possession; some have been influenced and guided by business leaders; others, by all classes ranging from bankers to peasant proprietors; generally, they have not been as wary of neighboring societies as have the migratory. In such a comparatively free atmosphere, writers have been more prone to express liberal ideas and urge reform, both within the society and in the field of international relations.

The expansive have maintained sharp divisions into classes or even castes; they have been ruled by court circles, military aristocracies or quasi-military cliques; also, they have been contemptuous of out-groups which they succeeded in subduing. Since the expansive hierarchies tended to regard war as an honorable profession, the authors whose loyalty they have commanded have generally avoided discussion of reform. Instead they have stood for heroism and military prowess or else, in some other way, have sought to justify the status quo.

Throughout our discussion, we have been concerned with the extent to which a society has engaged in conflict. We have noted that expansive societies have not only been the creation of conquest, but, by their very nature, have been more inclined than others to wage war. For one thing, membership in a court circle or aristocratic elite has been an exclusive privilege, and to justify their exalted positions, kings and nobles·have had to resort to arms in the event of affrontery to their states. For another, the privilege has imposed other obligations, of a civilian and purely social nature: the observing of all the amenities of rank, behavior, and attire. Such obligations have frequently been burdensome and even frustrating. Regimentation, inhibition, and frustration run counter to normal human inclination, and sooner or later find an outlet in hostility and aggression. Accordingly, among royal families and privileged upper classes of the expansive societies, channels for aggression have been sought and easily found.

Aside from the obligations and inhibitions which have spurred certain courts and military aristocracies alone, there have been additional sources of frustration that have affected all or most elements of expansive societies. In our treatment of the ancient world, we saw that from the feelings of guilt which followed periods of war or ruthless conquest several world religions evolved. Adherence to these world faiths entailed self-punishment as retribution for prevous conquest of and cruelty toward others. Such punishment of oneself was the accepted practice in Brahmanism, Buddhism, and, even more, in Christianity. But self-punishment—rigid conformity to doctrine, belief in the inherent defects or evil of man, and periods of fasting, sleeplessness, and abstinence from sexual activity —was, in turn, inhibiting and frustrating. Hence, in Europe especially, there was every inducement for not only the kings and nobles, but the knights and men-of-arms as well, to participate in wars and crusades. Indeed, it was hardly an accident that after the Inquisition was introduced in Spain and Portugal, these two societies became the leading aggressors in the West.

Even from the sixteenth century, when the Reformation exerted a profound impact, self-denial, if not self-punishment, though for state or commerce rather than for Church, was practiced in Protestant Europe. Thus, the way of life upheld in the northern European countries differed from that which arose farther south (Iberia excepted) under the milder influences of the Renaissance and Enlightenment. Accordingly, we made a second division of societies into those which practiced self-denial and those which were more tolerant of self-gratification.

It was among the middle classes of the expansive societies that this difference could be significant. For then the question as to whether or not a middle class practiced self-denial on behalf of the State had far reaching repercussions. Within the expansive social structures, the bourgeoisie, restricted in their opportunities and despised by the elites, felt bitterly resentful. If circumstances permitted a normal outlet for their hostility, as was the occasion in France under the Ancien Regime, a liberal bourgeois revolution would be the result. But if, through political and religious training and the absence of an Enlightenment, such antagonism was thwarted, it would be directed elsewhere. This was the case in the Germany of the Second Reich, where a vicious nationalistic reaction followed, a reaction which subsequently entailed a merciless subjugation of neighboring peoples.

Looking back over the centuries, we can readily discern two detrimental cycles: (1) expansion, self-punishment, frustration, also military aristocracy, inhibition, additional frustration, further expansion; and later, (2) self-denial amid a continued aristocratic order, a bitter but repressed burgher class, redirected hostility, still more expansion. This has been the calamitous sequence of processes which has exerted itself from late ancient, through medieval and early modern times, and well into the present age.

Today, very few of us regret that in Germany (at least, West Germany), Japan, and Italy, what were expansive societies have become interactive. But the discarding of the expansive socio-political order in these three countries, as well as in the Imperial Russian and Austrian empires, does not mean the termination of war. Although the major expansive societies, themselves the principal sources of past conflict, have been removed, there are still factors that can induce hostility. And this brings us to a consideration of the neo-migratory and interactive societies of the present day.

Within the neo-migratory, there is ground for frustration and, hence, potential hostility. To be sure, there is little in the way of a hereditary class system. Furthermore, the living standards of the common people, especially in Russia, are higher than they were in the pre-revolutionary expansive eras. In both countries, however, the authoritarianism and control of one's personal life are such as to induce feelings of animosity that would, of course, be directed toward others aside from those in power. Also, with the great stress that is placed on productivity as well as on personal conduct, such diverted hostility could be intensified. Already, an outlet for suppressed feelings has been seen in the activities of the Chinese Red Guards. But among the members of the Communist parties in both China and Russia, the need to preserve dignity prevents them from having such an outlet. Admittedly, membership in a highly integrated ruling body may give one a sense of belonging. But the feeling of being held strictly accountable for one's speech and actions could easily darken any sense of comradeship. Accordingly, certain members of the ruling circles could have the urge to promote aggressive foreign policies. The only compensation is that this urge would not be as prevalent as it was among the earlier nobles and warlords.

Within the interactive societies, there is less ground for animosity. Class distinctions are hardly rigid, while governments are by cautious bourgeoisie, which are interested primarily in peace and prosperity. Moreover, living standards are comparatively high, and people are far more free to express opinions than they have been in either the neo-migratory or former expansive societies. Still, there are factors that cause frustration and discontent.

Particularly in the societies influenced by the Reformation, there lingers a Puritanic quest to practice self-denial. Such can be noted in the feelings of guilt which many people have when enjoying leisure, good food, or sexual relations—even with their spouses. For the ghosts of ancient Roman imperialism, and of the later rebellion against the Church of Rome, still seem to haunt many persons today.

Owing, in turn, to the Puritan ban on deriving satisfaction from sensual pleasures, society seeks to provide other outlets. It encourages its members to "get ahead" and be "successful." In their move to scale the economic and social ladder, individuals are urged on by their families: sons are prompted to enter the leading universities and later secure top-level positions in prominent companies or attain to first rank in professions; daughters are induced to "marry well." Even recreation has come to have as its purpose the chance of meeting and knowing the "right people"; this motive is harnessed to the drive for success.

As long as an individual is successful, he will very likely be contented. But once this person senses that he is making very little progress in scaling the ladder, and if sufficiently ambitious, he may become embittered and seek an outlet for aggression. If engrossed in politics, he may join with other frustrated individuals and organize a group that would advocate an aggressive foreign policy. In so doing, he and his associates could play upon fear and mass hysteria and thus be in a position to influence public opinion.

Is there any solution to the frustration still common in the present day, a frustration attributable to either severe restriction or undue apprehension and also a failure to achieve? Is there any way in which life can be rendered more wholesome so as to eliminate the feelings of dejection that can induce hostility? While it would be difficult to eradicate these feelings completely, together with their sources, I believe that at least they can be minimized.

In setting forth solutions, I devote more space to what can be done in the interactive societies. My reason is that since they allow for greater freedom of expression than do the neo-migratory, they would be more flexible and receptive to ideas.

In the self-denying interactive societies, there could be, first of all, a change of attitude toward pleasure. Much could be done to remove the traditional guilt feelings which many people have when being leisurely and pursuing hobbies, having delicious repasts, or indulging in sex. To an extent, this could be accomplished through education and by competent educators. In the schools, instructors could show how the enjoyment of hobbies and of good food is as necessary to the human organism as are work and study. As for sex, a frank and scientific approach to the problem could also be made in the schools. Already, one interactive society—Sweden—is showing the way. Perhaps after two decades of Humanistic and scientific education, the emerging generation of John and Mary Does would not feel nearly as uneasy if spending several hours a day in leisure, dining on good food, or having intimate relations with their spouses.

Secondly, owing to the more relaxed atmosphere, there would be less in the way of personal rivalry and competition, particularly in the economic field. Here too, moreover, appropriate instruction could render valuable assistance. In the school, and also in the home and community, there could be less stress on competition, competition in the realms of scholarships, sports, and later, in that of the economy itself. As a corollary, there could be discarded the age-old tendency to envy and yet admire those who have been so "successful," particularly in business. Instead, the school, the home and the community could teach the younger generation the merit of finding work and social or cultural activity that is spiritually satisfying. Such instruction would have a far better chance of meeting with response if many new jobs were created, along with additional opportunities to enjoy leisure. For in this way, countless individuals would have greater hope of finding employment and activities that give psychic rewards.

Thus far, I have proposed ways in which society, as a whole, could broaden the outlook of its individual members. But then the individual himself could assist in this endeavor. Thirdly, therefore, I would suggest that he or she travel to neighboring or remote countries, and even to distant continents. If possible, he should try to learn the language of another society and become acquainted with its culture and way of life. Why? Because, in this way, he would be spared some of the tension which results from rivalry; he would have less of the guilt feelings that come from having failed to compete with a neighbor in his hometown. He would have a new and larger perspective and come to understand that life promises more than a mere struggle to "keep up with the Joneses." He might also learn that in a number of other societies, people do not feel as guilty when having leisure or a certain amount of pleasure. Even if he should feel some inconvenience in a different locality, the enlargement of human contacts, exposure to a new culture and enrichment of experience would be spiritually uplifting.

With widespread travel and communication becoming the order of the day among the interactive and even some developing societies, the neo-migratory would tend to discard their isolation. This they would do through their younger generations, which would be seeking to enjoy the good things of life, and such could be acquired through the exchange of information with the interactive world. To be sure, within the neo-migratory states, there could result a sharp conflict between the younger people, led by industrial managers and engineers, and the old guard political patriarchs and army chiefs. But in the struggle, the former would emerge victorious and do away with the severe restrictions to which they have been subjected. In effect, the neo-migratory societies would assume some of the characteristics of the interactive.

Such a vast increase in intersocietal travel and communication would itself be tantamount to a new wave of Interaction. It would resemble that which, in the early modern period, had carried on its crest the spirit of Humanism and the Renaissance. This present wave, however, would be far more encompassing. These potent interactive processes, so active in space, would be able to counteract any adverse effects of inhibition or frustration which could still be operating in time.

To be sure, self-denial and self-discipline, when practiced voluntarily by the people themselves rather than imposed by a regime, have had their merits. For, as we noted, they contributed much to political stability and economic growth. Such has been evidenced by the maintaining of long established and yet flexible governmental systems in Great Britain and the United States, and the phenomenal industrial development in Germany and Japan that raised the living standard in these two countries. Self-denial and self-discipline have also proved invaluable in moments of crisis. In the last great war, it was the British, Americans, and Russians who had the stamina and teamwork necessary for coping with the Axis Powers and bringing about their demise, a demise which could mark the end for eras of expansion.

Up to the present time, these beneficial results of self-discipline and self-denial have proved to be lasting. Therefore, we can afford to begin living in a more natural and relaxed manner. Such a change in habits and perspective can come about through education, travel and communication. Only in this way can our present existence be rendered more meaningful and wholesome. For was it not the very processes of interaction, both biological and physical, which, operating through divine law, and in space as well as in time, promoted evolution and brought forth life itself?

Bibliography

Aristotle. *Politics*. Translated by Benjamin Jowett, from *The Oxford Translation of Aristotle,* edited by W. D. Ross. Oxford: The Clarendon Press, 1921.

Atkins, G. G. and Braden, C. M. *Procession of the Gods.* New York: Harper & Row, 1936.

Bancroft, George. *History of the United States of America.* 6 vols. Boston: Little, Brown & Company, 1876.

Barker, E. H. *France of the French.* London: Sir Isaac Pitman & Sons, 1908.

Barton, George A. *The Religions of the World.* Chicago: University of Chicago Press, 1919.

Bede. *The Ecclesiastical History of the English Nation.* Translated by J. Stevens, revised by J. A. Giles. New York: Everyman's Library, 1958.

Bethune-Baker, J. F. *An Introduction to the Early History of Christian Doctrine.* London: Methuen & Company, Ltd., 1923.

The Bible. The Red Letter Edition of the King James version.

Blum, Jerome. *Lord and Peasant in Russia from the Ninth to the Nineteenth Century.* Princeton: Princeton University Press, 1961.

Bogardus, Emery S. *The Development of Social Thought.* New York: Longman's Green & Company, 1940.

Bowle, John. *Politics and Opinion in the Nineteenth Century.* London, Cape (Jonathan) Ltd., 1963.

Boxer, C. R. *Race Relations in the Portuguese Empire.* Oxford: The Clarendon Press, 1963.

Breasted, James H. *A History of Egypt from the Earliest Times to the Persian Conquest.* New York: Charles Scribner's Sons, 1937.

———. *The Dawn of Conscience.* New York: Charles Scribner's Sons, 1934.

Briffault, Robert. *The Mothers*. 3 vols. London: George Allen & Unwin, Ltd., 1927.

Brogan, Denis W. *The French Nation from Napoleon to Petain, 1815–1940*. New York: Harper & Row, 1958.

Buell, R. L. *The Native Problem in Africa*. 2 vols. New York: The Macmillan Company, 1928.

Bury, J. B. *A History of Greece*. Revised by C. Meiggs. London: Macmillan & Company, Ltd., 1930.

Cady, John F. *Southeast Asia: Its Historical Development*. New York: McGraw-Hill Book Company, 1964.

Caesar, Julius. *Commentaries on the Gallic and Civil Wars*. London: Henry G. Bohn, 1836.

Calvin, John. *Commentaries on the Four Last Books of Moses*. Translated by the Reverend Charles W. Bingham. Edinburgh: n.p., 1854.

———. *Memoirs of His Life and Writings*. Compiled by the Reverend Elijah Waterman. Hartford: n.p., 1813.

Carter, Jesse B. *The Religious Life of Ancient Rome*. Boston: Houghton Mifflin Company, 1911.

Ceram, C. W. *The Secret of the Hittites*. New York: Alfred A. Knopf, 1956.

Cobban, Alfred. *A History of Modern France*. 3 vols. New York: Penguin Books, 1965.

Codrington, R. H. *Melanesians*. Oxford: H. Frowde, The Clarendon Press, 1891.

Comte, Auguste. *System of Positive Polity*. 4 vols. London: Longman's Green & Company, 1875.

Coulton, G. C. *Life in the Middle Ages*. 4 vols. London: Cambridge University Press, 1930.

Creel, Herrlee. *Sinism: A Study of the Evolution of the Chinese World View*. Chicago: Open Court, 1929.

Croce, Benedetto. *A History of Italy*. Oxford: The Clarendon Press, 1929.

Daiches, David. *Literature and Society*. London: Victor Gollancz, Ltd., 1938.

Das, Santosh Kumar. *Economic History of Ancient India*. Calcutta: Mitra Press, 1925.

Dawson, William H. *German Life in Town and Country*. London: George Newnes, Ltd., 1901.

Debelius, William. *England*. Translated by Mary A. Hamilton. London: Cape (Jonathan), 1923.

Dhalla, M. N. *Zoroastrian Civilization*. New York: Oxford University Press, 1922.

Dostoevsky, Feodor. *The Possessed*. Translated by Constance Garnett. London: William Heinemann, 1914; New York: E. P. Dutton & Co., Everyman's Library, 1960.

Eckermann, Peter. *Conversation with Goethe*. New York: Everyman's Library, 1951.

Egerton, Hugh E. *A Short History of British Colonial Policy*. London: Methuen & Co., Ltd., 1913.

Epictetus. *The Discourses as Reported by Arrian, the Manual and Fragments*. 2 vols. Translated by W. A. Oldfather. The Loeb Classical Library, 1946.

Erasmus, Desiderius. *The Praise of Folly*. Translated with essay and commentary by H. H. Hudson. Princeton: Princeton University Press, 1951.

Euripides. *The Trojan Women*. Translated by Gilbert Murray. London: George Allen & Unwin, Ltd., 1919.

Fick, Richard. *The Social Organization in Northeast India in Buddha's Time*. Translated by Shishirkumar Maitra. Calcutta: University of Calcutta Press, 1920.

Fife, Robert H. *The German Empire between Two Wars*. New York: The Macmillan Company, 1918.

Finer, H. *Mussolini's Italy*. New York: Henry Holt & Co., 1935.

Finnegan, James. *Light from the Ancient Past*. 2 vols. Princeton: Princeton University Press, 1959.

Fitzgerald, C. P. *China: A Short Cultural History*. New York: Columbia University Press, 1923.

Fowler, W. Ward. *Social Life at Rome in the Age of Cicero*. New York: The Macmillan Company, 1907.

Frazer, James G. *The Fear of the Dead in Primitive Religion*. 3 vols. London: Macmillan & Co., Ltd., 1933.

Fustel de Coulanges, N. D. *The Ancient City: A Study on the Religion, Laws and Institutions of Greece and Rome*. Translated by Willard Small. Boston: Lothrop, Lee & Shephard Co., 1873.

Gershoy, Leo. *The French Revolution and Napoleon*. New York: Appleton & Company, 1933.

Glotz, Gustave. *Ancient Greece at Work: An Economic History of Greece.* New York: Alfred A. Knopf, 1926.

Gooch, George P. *Germany and the French Revolution.* London: Longman's Green & Company, 1920.

Gosses, F. *The Management of British Foreign Policy before the First World War.* Leiden: A. W. Sythoff's, 1948.

Hall, H. R. *Ancient History of the Near East.* London: Meuthen & Company, Ltd., 1950.

Halliday, William R. *Lectures on the History of Roman Religion.* Liverpool: Liverpool University Press, 1922.

Hara, Katsura. *An Introduction to the History of Japan.* New York: The Knickerbocker Press, 1920.

Harden, Donald B. *The Phoenicians: Ancient Peoples and Places.* London: Thames & Hudson, 1962.

Harrison, Jane Ellen. *Prolegomena to the Study of Greek Religion.* Cambridge: Cambridge University Press, 1908.

Hayes, Carleton J. H. *A Political and Cultural History of Modern Europe,* 2 vols. New York: The Macmillan Company, 1937.

Heiden, Konrad. *The History of National Socialism.* New York: Alfred A. Knopf, 1935.

Hollis, A. C. *The Nandi.* Oxford: The Clarendon Press, 1909.

Horace, *Odes.* 2 vols. Translated by Philip Francis. London: A. J. Valpy, 1831.

Jebb, R. C. *Greek Literature.* London: Macmillan & Company, Ltd., 1913.

Johnson, A. H. *Europe in the Sixteenth Century.* London: Rivington's Press, 1923.

Johnson, Samuel. *The Rambler.* New York: Everyman's Library, 1953.

Jones, Tom B. *An Introduction to Hispanic American History.* New York and London: Harper & Brothers, 1939.

Junod, H. A. *Life of a South African Tribe.* 2 vols. London: Macmillan & Company, Ltd., 1927.

Kautsky, Karl. *Foundations of Christianity.* Translated by Henry F. Mins. New York: S. A. Russel Company, 1953.

King, Bolton. *A History of Italian Unity.* 2 vols. London: Nisbet & Company, Ltd., 1924.

Kitto, John. *Palestine from the Patriarchal Age to the Present*

Time, in *World's Best Histories.* London: Cooperative Publishing Society, 1920.

Kulski, W. W. *The Soviet Regime: Communism in Practice.* Syracuse, N.Y.: Syracuse University Press, 1956.

Kuo, Ping-Chia. *China: New Age and New Outlook.* New York: Alfred A. Knopf, 1936.

Landtman, G. *The Kiwai Papuans of British New Guinea.* London: Macmillan & Company, Ltd., 1927.

Latourette, Kenneth S. *The Chinese: Their History and Culture.* New York: The Macmillan Company, 1947.

Lee, Mabel Ping hua. *Economic History of China.* New York: Columbia University Press, 1923.

Lewis, John W. *Leadership in Communist China.* Ithaca, N.Y.: Cornell University Press, 1963.

Lin Yutang. *My Country and My People.* New York: John Day & Company, 1935.

Lockart, R. Bruce. *Retreat from Glory.* London: G. Putnam & Sons, Ltd., 1934.

Loeb, Jacques. *Forced Movements, Tropisms, and Animal Conduct.* New York: J. B. Lippincott, 1919.

Louis, Paul. *Ancient Rome at Work.* London: Kegan Paul, Trench, Trubner & Company, Ltd., 1927.

Luther, Martin. *Open Letter to the Christian Nobility.* Translated by C. M. Jacobs *et al,* in *Works.* Philadelphia: Fortress Press, 1916.

————. *Letters of Spiritual Counsel,* in *Library of Christian Classics.* Vol. XVIII, Philadelphia: Westminster Press, 1957.

Lynch, Hannah. *French Life in Town and Country.* London: George Newnes, Ltd., 1901.

Macaulay, Thomas B. *Speeches on Politics and Literature.* New York: Everyman's Library, 1917.

Malinowsky, B. *Crime and Custom in Savage Society.* London: Routledge & Kegan Paul, Ltd., 1961.

————. *Sex and Repression in Savage Society.* London: Routledge & Kegan Paul, Ltd.; New York: Harcourt, Brace & World, Inc., 1953.

Mavor, James. *An Economic History of Russia.* 2 vols. New York: The Macmillan Company, 1937.

Mayer, Joseph B. *A Sketch of Ancient Philosophy from Thales* to *Cicero*. Cambridge, U. K.: Cambridge University Press, 1912.

Menninger, Karl A. *The Human Mind*. New York: Alfred A. Knopf, 1945.

Michelet, Jules. *A Historical View of the French Revolution*. Translated by C. Cocks. London: George Bell & Sons, 1912.

Mill, John Stuart. *Utilitarianism, Liberty and Representative Government*. New York: Everyman's Library, 1944.

Milton, John. *A Second Defense of the English People*. Translated by Helen North, in *Complete Prose Works*, Vol. IV, Part I, edited by Don M. Wolfe. New Haven: Yale University Press, 1966.

Mommsen, Theodore. *The History of Rome*. 2 vols. Translated by the Reverend William P. Dickson. London: Richard Bentley & Sons, 1872.

Montaigne, Michel de. *The Essays*. Charles Cotton's translation edited by C. Carew Haslitt (Bohn) in *Great Books of the World*, Vol. 25. London: George Bell & Sons, Ltd., 1952.

Morison, Samuel E. and Commager, Henry S. *The Growth of the American Republic*. 2 vols. New York: Oxford University Press, 1937.

Mornet, Daniel. *A Short History of French Literature*. Translated by C. A. Choquette and Christian Gauss. New York: F. S. Crofts & Company, 1935.

Murray, Gilbert. *Euripides and His Age*. New York: Henry Holt & Company, 1913.

Nansen, F. *Eskimo Life*. Translated by W. Archer. London: Longman's Green & Company, 1893.

Nietzsche, Friedrich. *The Will to Power*. Translated by A. M. Ludovici from *Complete Works*, edited by Oscar Levi. London: George Allen & Unwin, Ltd., 1924.

Nihongi. Translated by W. G. Aston. London: George Allen & Unwin, Ltd., 1956.

Nillson, M. *History of Greek Religion*. Oxford: The Clarendon Press, 1925.

Nitobe, Inazo. *Bushido: The Soul of Japan*. Tokyo: Teibi Publishing Company, 1908.

————. *Lectures on Japan*. Tokyo: Kenkyusha, Ltd., 1936.

Origen. *Writings*. 2 vols. Translated by the Reverend Frederick Crombie. Edinburgh: T. T. Clark, 1910.

Owen, Francis. *The Germanic People*. New York: Brookline Association, 1960.

Oxford History of India. Oxford: The Clarendon Press, 1923.

Pares, Bernard. *A History of Russia*. London: Cape (Jonathan) Ltd., 1949.

Pareto, Vilfredo. *The Mind and Society*. 4 vols. New York: Harcourt, Brace & World, Inc., 1935.

Parrington, Vernon L. *Main Currents in American Thought*. Three volumes. New York: Harcourt, Brace & World, Inc., 1930.

Petrarch's Secret. Translated by William H. Draper. London: Chatto & Windus, 1911.

Powell, T. G. E. *The Celts*. London: Thames & Hudson, 1958.

Pratt, J. W. *America's Colonial Experiment*. New York: Prentice-Hall, Inc., 1950.

Pritchard, H. H. *Polynesian Reminiscences*. London: n.p., 1856.

Prudentius. *Works*. 2 vols. Translated by H. J. Thomson. The Loeb Classical Library, 1949.

Randall, John H. *The Making of the Modern Mind*. Boston: Houghton Mifflin Company, 1940.

Rank, Otto. *The Trauma of Birth*. London: Routledge & Kegan Paul, Ltd., 1929.

Reischauer, Edwin O. *Japan, Past and Present*. Tokyo: Charles E. Tuttle Company, 1964.

Renou, Louis. *Religions of Ancient India*. London: Athlone Press, 1953.

Roberts, Stephen H. *The History of French Colonial Policy, 1870–1925*. 2 vols. London: Frank Case & Company, Ltd., 1963.

Robinson, Edwin A. *The Man Against the Sky*, in *Collected Poems*. New York: The Macmillan Company, 1954.

Rostovtzeff, Michael. *Social and Economic History of the Hellenistic World*. 3 vols. Oxford: The Clarendon Press, 1941.

———. *Social and Economic History of the Roman Empire*. Oxford: The Clarendon Press, 1926.

Rousseau, Jean Jacques. *The Social Contract and Discourses*. New York: Everyman's Library, 1949.

Russell, Bertrand. *History of Western Philosophy and its Connection with Political and Social Circumstances from the*

Earliest Times to the Present Day. London: George Allen & Unwin, Ltd., 1962.

Russell, Phillips. *Jefferson, Champion of the Free Mind*. New York: Dodd, Mead & Company, 1956.

Samaddar, J. N. *Lectures on the Economic Condition of Ancient India*. Calcutta: University of Calcutta Press, 1922.

Sansome, George. *A History of Japan to 1334*. London: The Cresset Press, 1958.

————. *Japan: A Short Cultural History*. London: The Cresset Press, 1936.

Saunders, E. D. *Buddhism in Japan*. Philadelphia: University of Pennsylvania Press, 1964.

Schuman, Frederick L. *Hitler and the Nazi Dictatorship*. London: R. Hale & Company, 1936.

Scott-Robertson, G. *Kafirs of the Hindu Kush*. London: Lawrence Bullen, Ltd., 1896.

Sergeant, Lewis. *The Franks*. London: T. Fisher Unwin, 1898.

Shull, A. F., *et al. Principles of Animal Biology*. New York: McGraw-Hill Book Company, 1934.

Simmons, E. J., ed. *Continuity and Change in Russian and Soviet Thought*. Cambridge, Mass.: Harvard University Press, 1955.

Sinha, Jadunath. *A History of Indian Philosophy*. 2 vols. Calcutta: Central Book Agency, 1956.

Sircar, D. C. *Inscriptions of Asoka*. *Delhi*s Publications Division, Ministry of Information and Broadcasting, 1957.

Smith, Denis Mack. *Italy: A Modern History*. Ann Arbor: University of Michigan Press, 1959.

Smith, Preserved. *A History of Modern Culture*. 2 vols. New York: Henry Holt & Company, 1934.

————. *The Age of the Reformation*. 2 vols. New York: Henry Holt & Company, 1920.

Sources of the Chinese Tradition, Sources of the Indian Tradition, and *Sources of the Japanese Tradition,* from *Introduction to Oriental Civilization,* in *Records of Civilization: Sources and Studies*. Edited by W. T. de Bary. New York: Columbia University Press, 1958.

Spencer, Baldwin, and Gillen, F. J. *The Native Tribes of Central Australia*. London: Macmillan & Company, 1899.

Sproat, G. M. *Scenes and Studies of Savage Life.* London: Smith & E., 1868.

Stern, Jacques. *The French Colonies, Past and Future.* New York: Didier Publishing Company, 1944.

Storry, Richard. *A History of Modern Japan.* New York: Penguin Books, 1960.

Sundstrom, Harold W. *Indonesia: Its People and Politics.* Tokyo: The Hokuseido Press, 1957.

Tacitus. *The Complete Works.* Translated by A. J. Church and W. J. Brodribb. New York: The Modern Library, 1942.

Taine, Hippolyte A. *Notes on England.* Translated by Edward Hyams. London: Thames & Hudson, 1957; The Hague: N. V. Drukkery Levison, 1957.

Takekoshi, Y. *The Economic Aspects of the History of Civilization in Japan.* 3 vols. London: Dawsons, Pall Mall, Ltd., 1936.

Tawney, Richard H. *Religion and the Rise of Capitalism.* London: John Murray, 1927.

Taylor, Henry O. *The Medieval Mind.* 2 vols. London: Macmillan & Company, Ltd., 1914.

Thompson, George. *Aeschylus and Athens.* London: Lawrence & Wishart, 1941.

Thompson, James W. and Johnson, Edgar N. *An Introduction to Medieval Europe 300–1500.* New York: W. W. Norton & Company, 1937.

Thurston, E. *Ethnographic Notes in Southern India.* Madras: Probstain & Company, 1907.

Tocqueville, Alexis de. *Journeys to England and Ireland.* Translated by George Lawrence and K. P. Mayer. New Haven: Yale University Press, 1958.

Tolstoi, Leo. *Essays and Letters.* Translated by Aylmer Maude. Oxford: H. Frowde, The Clarendon Press, 1911.

———. *The End of the Age.* Translated by V. Tchertkoff and I. F. Mayo. London: William Heinemann, 1906.

Treitschke, Heinrich von. *Politics.* 2 vols. Translated by Blanche Dugdale and Torben de Bille. London: Constable & Company, Ltd., 1916.

Trevelyan, George M. *English Social History: A Survey of Six Centuries from Chaucer to Queen Victoria.* London: Longman's Green & Company, 1965.

Troeltsch, Ernst. *The Social Teaching of the Christian Churches.* Translated by O. Wyon. London: George Allen & Unwin, Ltd., 1939.

Vaughan, C. E. *Studies in the History of Political Philosophy.* 2 vols. Manchester: Manchester University Press, 1939.

Virgil. *Georgics, from Works.* 2 vols. Translated by H. Rushton Fairclough. The Loeb Classical Library, 1956.

Vitalis, Odoricus. *The Ecclesiastical History of England and Normandy.* 3 vols. Translated by T. Forrester. London: Henry G. Bohn, 1854.

Voltaire. *The Philosophical Dictionary.* London: Jacques & Company, 1802.

Webb, Sidney, and Webb, Beatrice. *Soviet Communism: A New Civilization.* 2 vols. London: Longman's Green & Co., Ltd., 1937.

Webster, Hutton. *Taboo.* Stanford: Stanford University Press, 1942.

Wendel, Barrett. *The France of Today.* New York: Charles Scribner & Sons, 1907.

Westermarck, Edward. *The Origin and Development of the Moral ideas.* 2 vols. London: Macmillan & Co., 1906.

Whitman, Walt. *Complete Poetry, Selected Prose and Letters.* Edited by Emory Holloway. London: The Nonesuch Press, 1938.

Wile, Frederick W. *The Men around the Kaiser: The Makers of Modern Germany.* London: William Heinemann, 1914.

Zetkin, Clara. *Reminiscences of Lenin.* London: Modern Books Company, 1929.

Zielinski, Thaddeus. *The Religion of Ancient Greece.* Translated by George R. Noyes. London: Humphrey Milford, Oxford University Press, 1926.

Zimmern, Helen. *Italy of the Italians.* London: Pitman & Sons, Ltd., 1910.

Index

239